REIMAGINING
SUCCESS

*Manifesting Happiness
and Fulfillment*

MAUREEN FALLON-CYR, LCSW

Reimagining Success:
Manifesting Happiness and Fulfillment

Copyright © 2023 by Maureen Fallon-Cyr, LCSW

Printed in the United States of America

Hardcover ISBN: 978-1-961624-27-6
Paperback ISBN: 978-1-961624-28-3
Ebook ISBN: 978-1-961624-31-3
Library of Congress Control Number: 2023951471

DartFrog Plus is the hybrid publishing imprint
of DartFrog Books, LLC.
301 S. McDowell St.
Suite 125-1625
Charlotte, NC 28204
www.DartFrogBooks.com

Advance Praise for Reimagining Success

"Success is an elusive concept, never more so than during these uncertain times. Maureen Fallon-Cyr has given us a gift that can guide us to the goal of authentic, meaningful success. Utilizing friendly, understandable language, real-life examples, and decades of experience, she and her husband Mark—both dear colleagues of mine—provide a therapeutic system that helps us achieve True Success. Mother Teresa once said: "I used to believe that prayer changes things, but now I believe that prayer changes us, and we change things." Similarly, Maureen underscores that we are the prime movers in creating a meaningful, fulfilling life and her model helps us utilize our own inner resources to achieve our own True Success."

—Mark Albanese, M.D.,
Medical Director, Massachusetts Physician Health Services
and Assistant Professor of Psychiatry,
Harvard Medical School/Cambridge Health Alliance

"It is my pleasure to write these words inviting you to go on a journey with Maureen Fallon-Cyr to explore *Reimagining Success: Manifesting Happiness and Fulfillment.* As a meditation teacher, I've known Maureen for many years, initially through sitting on meditation retreats at Spirit Rock Meditation Center where I teach. I have always been impressed by her courage, willingness, and honesty to explore the inner world, including the most vulnerable parts of the psyche, in the quest to find true peace and freedom. As a beloved meditation teacher with strong meditation practice and a deep psychology background, she expertly guides students in accessing and awakening their own understanding, love, and inner peace. Based on their decades of experience, Maureen and her husband Mark have developed a model that can be applied to anyone, no matter what their psychological or spiritual background, or field of interest might be. Through engaging anecdotes and conversations with her clients, as well as personal sharing of her own story, she leads the reader through a journey to help them discover their own gifts and develop the areas where more attention will lead to True Success—not the material success that most people are chasing, but a success resulting in a sense of genuine fulfillment and ease."

—James Baraz,
Co-Founder, Spirit Rock Meditation Center,
and author of *Awakening Joy: Ten Steps
That Will Put You on the Road to Real Happiness*

"As an educator in alternative schools and teacher trainer for over thirty years, I have worked with Maureen and Mark Fallon-Cyr in a number of educational and clinical settings. The integrity and wisdom they bring to working with others gives me the utmost respect for their work. Their lifelong development of practices, strategies and skills presented in the True Success program offers a profoundly different approach to understanding ourselves and our world. In *Reimagining Success: Manifesting Happiness and Fulfillment,* Maureen brings teachings and healing practices that give us a new way to walk in the world. Through tools, strategies, skills, and experiential activities, she shows us how to live more authentically and discover our True Nature. When people change, the world changes. This book has the power to change people."

—Eric Larsen, M.Ed.,
retired public school teacher,
and Founder of the Discovery Program

"In *Reimagining Success: Manifesting Happiness and Fulfillment*, Maureen Fallon-Cyr has created a revolutionary way of envisioning and working toward success, providing a robust and enlivening roadmap to examining seven individual domains in our lives and their roles in our individual and collective satisfaction. I am inspired by her schema to identify the strengths and areas of growth in these domains, and to use the work to bring my true essence into everything I do, as a professor, activist, family member, and writer. Leaders, teachers, and helpers everywhere will find particular value in her framework, which will enable them to step into their roles with more courage, confidence, and compassion."

—Susan Marine, PhD.,
Professor of Education and Vice Provost,
Merrimack College

"I have had the privilege of knowing Maureen and Mark Fallon-Cyr for over 30 years. Having trained together at a Harvard teaching hospital in Boston, working with underserved persons with severe and persistent mental illness, I witnessed the birth of their life-long dedication to the mental well-being of all people, regardless of their backgrounds or life experiences. Since then, I have watched Maureen hone her therapeutic skills, integrating traditional and non-traditional approaches to healing with a unique approach. The True Success model encompasses a wholistic vision of healing and wellness that has the potential to be life altering for those who chose to follow this path. Maureen's warmth, along with the specific tools included in *Reimagining Success: Manifesting Happiness and Fulfillment* make it an approachable and engaging read. As a psychiatrist who treats patients, teaches psychiatry, and engages with the community, I see this work as important and empowering."

—Roxanne Bartel, M.D., psychiatrist

"With elegant simplicity and clarity, and always encouraging kindness and curiosity, Maureen steers us toward uncovering and releasing our limiting inner stories, the "mental formations," that cause unnecessary suffering and hinder our success in life. In a process that feels both natural and profound, we are led to access, then live from our Essence—the place inside that is calm and resourced, even as life brings its challenges. *True Success* rings true, reverberating clear as a bell."

—Dr. Cedar Barstow,
Hakomi mindfulness-based somatic psychology trainer,
Founder, Right Use of Power Institute, and author
of *Right Use of Power: The Heart of Ethics*

Disclaimer

This book contains general information about psychology, mindfulness, and somatic healing methods and should not be a substitute for the skill, knowledge, and experience of a qualified medical or mental health professional. The information presented is not medical or psychological advice. As such, the author, publisher, and their distributors are not responsible for adverse effects or consequences resulting from the use of the information in this book.

*Dedicated to those seeking to embody
a truly successful life.*

Table of Contents

Preface

In today's world you can't escape the trappings of success. Media feeds, television, and self-help books continuously entice us to boost our success in finance, parenting, weight loss, exercise, fashion, aging, and even meal preparation. So why would I write a book that speaks to success? Because I was *tired*. Over the years, I worked hard to be successful in many arenas, only to feel unsuccessful and unfulfilled. No matter which success program I ventured into, I quickly slipped back into old habits, disheartened and let down—I wasn't "changing for the better," I wasn't manifesting the "me" I wanted to be, and when I did achieve a goal, I often suffered from imposter syndrome—I could barely own my achievements or was unable to savor the joy that came with the accolades. I was living a generally good life, but I wasn't feeling *successful*.

As a psychotherapist, I was witnessing the same scenario in my practice. I spent years helping people achieve their ideal of a successful life, watching as my clients attained their goals, only to realize that their happiness and satisfaction didn't last. They had the right job and acquired all the things that were supposed to make them happy, yet they still felt unsatisfied, discontent, or "not good enough." Clearly, the key to a meaningful, satisfying life lay outside achievement.

Intrigued by this phenomenon—both in my clients and in my own life—I spent years studying and then teaching mindfulness and meditation, entrusting that the peace and ease found in stillness would soothe our collective restlessness. Yet I encountered a similar roadblock... With mindfulness practices, I often saw that people could relax their mind and enjoy illuminating experiences, but as soon as they got off the cushion, they were plagued by difficulties—they were still agitated, impulsive, or overwhelmed by the stressors in their life, a condition not unlike the backslides I saw with our current success programs. I began to wonder... Beyond relaxation and soothing, could mindfulness be used to heal our busy, flustered mind? Was it possible to release the worrisome part of ourself so that we could relax and be content with life?

To answer this question, I began weaving my mindfulness and psychology practices together. Mindfulness allowed me to settle and relax my system, while psychology showed me the worries, fears, and doubts that needed releasing in order to create a sense of well-being and contentment. Using a practice of mindfulness to release my fears and doubts, I soon experienced a healing and ease I had not felt before. I felt happier, more relaxed, and I was enjoying more success in my life—I was making better choices, connecting with others more authentically and warmly, and I found that I was a lot less ruffled by stress and disturbances. When I did have successes, I was able to own them and savor them, leaving me feeling fulfilled in many areas of my life.

This new experience of successful living is what my husband Mark and I began to call *True Success*. True Success is the success we long for; when we are no longer burdened by our fears and doubts, we discover the inner ease and clarity of our own True Nature, that which expresses our passions and unique skills in ways that promote happiness and contentment. In our True Nature, we return to the aliveness, confidence, and freedom we had as young children, connected to a deep inner presence that can guide us in making insightful, inspired choices that lead to authentic, joyful living. With True Success, we manifest the life we have always wanted to live, the life we are meant to live.

This book is an invitation for you to discover your own True Success. Throughout the book, we offer fresh perspectives, new ways of connecting deeply with yourself, and practices that can help you release your fears, worries, and doubts so you can rediscover your True Nature. Many people have already engaged with True Success, finding a deep healing that allows them to engage their life in fresh ways, bringing them joy, fulfillment, and the feeling of a life well-lived.

The work I present here is crafted out of many teachings and trainings I have received over decades. I gratefully stand upon the shoulders and wisdom of many teachers and mentors. My work is seasoned by the theories of psychology, social work, and trauma work, as well as the Hakomi Method, Buddhism, and mindfulness trainings. If you are familiar with these traditions, you may recognize their presence in my work.

I also want to note that the True Success teachings are presented in the format of psychotherapy sessions. Over the years, Mark and I have offered these teachings in workshops, classes, as well as psychotherapy sessions, but for simplicity, I'm offering these teachings in a therapy format as it presents a clear, distilled arena that illustrates the unfolding of the healing process. While the healing scenarios are true, I have changed identities and identifying conditions of students and clients in order to protect their privacy. In gratitude, I offer deep appreciation to those I have worked with over these decades. They have trusted me with their vulnerability and their wounds, and their healing process has informed the heart of this work.

Finally, the sessions portrayed have been condensed for the sake of brevity. In truth, healing is an up and down journey that requires time and patience. It takes time to heal and become our true self, yet it is an investment well made—for in our healing, we return to the essence of who we truly are; wise, caring, joyful people, bound for success. If you find yourself inspired to live a truly successful life, one built on your inherent goodness and natural abilities, I invite you to rediscover your own True Nature.

Section One

Reimagining Success

What is True Success?

Everyone dreams of a successful life. While the markers may look different for each of us—having a cool car...owning a house...starting a business...finding true love...or a combination of these—they point to a similar hope and aspiration: Our success should bring ease, contentment, and happiness, confirming to ourselves and the world that we are a "good" person, deserving of prosperity and blessings. We may chase the American Dream or work hard to amass fortune, fame, power, or status, convinced that when we reach our goal, happiness will be ours. But even when we realize our goals and dreams, are we living a truly successful life? We may find that our success doesn't bring the ease and contentment we dreamed of. We may not feel "good enough," despite our achievements, or we may struggle with personal issues—our success didn't resolve our addiction, our intimacy issues, our anxiety, or our anger outbursts. How can we come to live a healthy, satisfying, meaningful life—in other words, a truly successful life? Intrigued by this question, my husband Mark and I set out to find the answer.

Many years ago when Mark was in medical school, he came face-to-face with this question in a way that would change our lives. Back then, Mark had his own ideas of success—he had worked hard putting himself through college and medical school, and he was hoping to earn a medical internship at a prestigious hospital. When Yale University offered him a spot at one of their teaching hospitals just outside New York City, he was overjoyed. A well-respected hospital, the facility treated many business tycoons, politicians, and socialites—people who had definitely "made it" in the high-stakes arena of Manhattan. Mark was excited to join the program as he knew he would get top training and exceptional experience. What he couldn't imagine was that he was about to learn far more than medical skills. Mark was about to learn what it means to be truly successful.

A few weeks into his training, a new patient was presented to the medical team. A Wall Street financier had been admitted with complications from a cancer that was ending his life. As they were about to enter the room, the attending physician turned to the group, "He still has a lot of sway in New York, so I expect you to treat him with the utmost respect."

Mark had been assigned to follow this patient, so he was eager to meet this towering figure. However, when they walked in the room, he was taken aback. The skeletal figure lying in the bed looked nothing like a powerful Manhattan financier. The man was shrunken, pale, and weak, and the tubes and machines connected to him seemed to take up more space in the room than he did.

Later that morning, after finishing his rounds, Mark went back to his patient's room to formally introduce himself. Having already decided to specialize in psychiatry, Mark had a keen interest in understanding his patients' inner world as he believed our inner world builds the life we live. Standing outside the patient's room, he took a moment to compose himself, then stepped in, introducing himself with a warm handshake and the respect he knew this man was accustomed to. Taking his hand, the man beamed at Mark, looking genuinely grateful for the visit.

"You can call me Walter. Glad to make your acquaintance. I don't get many visitors here; well, at least not the ones I want to see!" He rolled his eyes with a gentle mirth, and Mark chuckled. He liked Walter's candor and his easy manner. Smiling at each other, they marked the beginning of a friendship that would brighten Walter's last days, bringing them both a precious gift.

Following their first visit, anytime Mark peeked into the room, Walter would light up: "Come in! Come in!" Soon, a sweet ritual developed: Mark would ask Walter about his health and Walter would shoo him off dismissively. "I don't want talk about that. Let me tell you about the time I..." launching into a story about his New York glory days.

"I'm telling you Mark, I had it all! The women, the parties... I've eaten the best meals, stayed at the best resorts, played on the best golf links and had the best *partners*, if you know what I mean. Oh, the adventures I've had!" Walter's tales were exotic, filled with glamorous escapades and intriguing glimpses into the backroom deals of the rich and famous, many of which involved high drama and some questionable legal dealings. For Mark, it was very entertaining, but deep down he couldn't help but sense that there was an emptiness lurking behind Walter's euphoria.

A couple of weeks into Walter's stay, one cold and rainy afternoon, Mark stopped in for his usual visit. On this day, Walter wasn't his jovial self, but instead he was pensive and irritated. Quietly, Mark sat down next to his bed and waited. He decided he would let Walter begin.

After a long silence, Walter turned to Mark. "They're not coming. My wife's not coming, my son's not coming. And why should they? All I ever cared about was the money, the fun, the power..." Closing his eyes, he shook his head in disgust, sighing dishearteningly. Mark sat quietly, sensing there was more.

The next moment, Walter's eyes flew open: "Actually, that's not true!" His voice was edgy, but clear. "That's all my father ever wanted! All he cared about was money, women, and power." Glancing over at Mark, he smiled, as if relieved to have discovered this truth. But just as quickly, his face fell and he turned away, staring at the rain-streaked window as if absorbed in another place and time. When he spoke again, his voice was bitter. "Do you know what that asshole said to me? He told me, 'You're not a real man, until you make your first million.' Can you believe that?!" He grumbled, clearly annoyed with the cruelty of it.

"When I graduated from Harvard, I told him that I wanted to take some time off...maybe go into the Peace Corps. He was disgusted with the idea. He told me that he'd 'cut me off' if I went through with it. God, I hated him! But I was always trying to impress the son-of-a-bitch, even after he died."

Mark was imagining Walter as a young man, trying to do something meaningful, yet desperate for his father's approval, bumping up against that hard-edge. He was trying to think of what to say, when Walter pressed on.

"I ended up just like him... When my wife wanted kids, all I wanted was the 'perfect life.' For me, that was growing my wealth, traveling, being at the right parties, and being in the rooms where the big decisions were being made. The thought of dragging a kid along...let's just say that it wasn't in my plans. I couldn't see the importance of it." He closed his eyes, resting a moment, looking tired and burdened. When he continued, his voice was somber. "When my son was born, I never paid him much attention. And I told my wife, 'One's enough!' I wanted the freedom to pursue my work, my networking, and my net worth." He cringed, hearing his last words. Looking embarrassed, he turned away from Mark and stared out the window again, watching the rain in silence.

When he continued, he avoided Mark's gaze, speaking more to the window than to Mark. "When I got older, I had this idea that I was going to give my son the business—you know, as part of my *legacy*..." He rolled his eyes, annoyed at his pretentiousness. "But when I asked him to come on board, he practically spit in my face. He actually screamed at me, 'You're not going to use me like you use everyone else!'" Wincing, he quietly added, "He lives in Europe with his wife and kids now. I don't see much of him."

Softly, Mark said, "I'm sorry you don't get to see them." Walter looked up. "Yeah, me too."

A few days later, Mark walked into Walter's room to find him lying quietly in the dark. "Would you like me to turn the lights on?" he offered. "No. It's fine," Walter responded. "I like it better this way." Mark sat down, ready to offer whatever Walter needed.

"I checked all the boxes, Mark. I played out the whole damn script—the money, the power, the prestige, and the whole time I was barking up the wrong tree. I missed all the important stuff that really matters. The shitty thing is, I see it all now and I don't have the time to make it up to anyone—not to my son, my wife, anyone..." Tears rolled down his face as the last of his façade fell away. Touched by Walter's grief, Mark reached over and gently rested his hand on his arm. With the warmth of the gesture, Walter began sobbing and the room filled with the agony of his hard-won realization.

Sitting quietly, Mark was managing his own tears now. Over the past weeks, he had grown quite fond of Walter. He loved his lively spirit and had been deeply moved by Walter's insights and his softening. He was reflecting on Walter's transformation and his great loss, when he startled—Walter had grabbed him by the arm and was fixing him with a fierce, urgent look on his face.

"Don't make the same mistake I did, Mark! Do you hear me?! I'd give it all away—the money...the power...everything...just to have another chance. I would do it all differently! I'd join the Peace Corps, love my family, and I'd use my money to make a difference in this world. Promise me you'll do something meaningful! Love the people in your life! And don't let anyone pull you away from that!" He held Mark's eyes, imploring him, "Promise me you won't make the same mistakes I made!"

Shocked, Mark heard himself promising that he would dedicate his life to the important things—he would keep love in the forefront of his life, he would live true to his values, and he would pursue his passions and dreams.

The rest of that day went by in a haze. Unable to shake Walter's plea, Mark played the exchange over and over in his head as he attended to his duties. It was only on the walk home that evening that he finally had a chance to reflect on Walter's words. Here was a man who'd "had it all;" he had been highly successful in all the traditional realms of success and yet at the end of his life, he was saying, *if you don't love well and live your truth, it's all for naught.*

Reaching home, Mark walked into his living room and stretched out on the couch, closing his eyes to rest a moment. As his mind quieted, he felt deep gratitude for Walter and his final teaching. Transformed by their exchange that day, Mark made a vow to himself. He would learn what it takes to live a truly successful life—an authentic, meaningful life—and he would share it with others.

*   *   *

Throughout the remainder of his internship, Mark found that Walter wasn't the only one to arrive at this deeper truth. Many of his patients—other business tycoons, politicians, and socialites—secretly confided to Mark that they had gotten the formula wrong. As these men and women grappled with illnesses that threatened their life, many told Mark that given another chance, they would do it differently—they would live authentically, champion the values that were dear to their heart, do what they loved, and importantly, they would do whatever it took to love others fully.

Many of Mark's patients had fulfilled what would be considered a successful life—financial well-being and physical comfort—yet this didn't satisfy their yearnings for a meaningful life. Many longed for deeper family connection. Many wished that they had developed the courage to follow their passions and dreams. Others wished that they had lived authentically, expressing their true values and beliefs. What these men and women were pointing to was an expression of *self-fulfillment*, not *self-satisfaction*. As humans, we deeply yearn to experience the significance of our life, share our wisdom,

> As humans, we deeply yearn to experience the significance of our life, share our wisdom, connect with our deepest Source, and embody Love.

connect with our deepest Source, and embody Love. This "fuller life" that people described is what Mark and I came to call *True Success*. It was clear that this "fuller life" was the key to a vibrant, meaningful life, but we wondered...what are the elements that make for truly successful living?

Success vs True Success

Following his internship, Mark went on to his medical residency where he and I met when we were assigned to work on the same psychiatric unit at a Harvard training hospital. I was interning in psychiatric social work; he was in his first year of training in adult psychiatry. As we worked together, we discovered that we shared a common passion: Beyond treating our patients' disorders, we wanted to empower our patients to build healthy, stable lives so they could pursue the passions and dreams that would bring them a meaningful and fulfilling life. Inspired in part by Walter's experience, we began exploring what a truly successful life might entail. We read through numerous books and studies and surveyed popular programs promoting success. But over and over the sources referenced wealth, status, and power as markers of success, the very measures Walter had found unfulfilling.

Not finding what we were looking for in books and programs, we began interviewing people, hoping to uncover what defines a happy and fulfilling life. We interviewed those who were striving to be successful, as well as those who had felt they had "made it." As we deepened into our conversations with people, an interesting pattern emerged: Many told us that *if they could succeed in one or two important areas of their life, they would be "successful" and their life would be carefree.* For example, once they got their business off the ground, they would have the resources to fix all their problems. But when we asked those who had attained their dream—those who had the money, the great home, the partner they wanted, and other standards of success—if they were happy and satisfied, most admitted that something was missing, and many of them were still struggling with feelings of disappointment or deficiency.

Walter's story shows us what commonly happens when we attempt to secure the conventional markers of success. Often, we overfocus on a chosen area of development (build up a business, attain a goal, gain preferred status, etc.), while we ignore or abandon other parts of our life that are not working as well. I remember one lawyer who told me with full conviction, "As soon as I make partner, everything will be great!" But in truth, he had come into therapy because he was suffering from depression and prescription drug abuse, symptoms of his unresolved trauma. No amount of money or status was going to lessen his suffering.

Perhaps you've found yourself believing this idea—that once you attain a particular goal, you'll have it made and you will be "successful" and happy. Once you lose weight and get in shape, you'll find that partner you've always dreamed of. Once you finish school or get into the "right" graduate program, you'll have proof that you're "smart enough." When you get the promotion, your anxiety will go away. When you find the perfect job, you'll be happy and satisfied.

But as we saw with Walter, success in one area of life doesn't guarantee success across our life. Walter was gifted in business matters and making money, but that didn't translate to happiness in his personal life. In truth, all of us are gifted in some areas, but not others. You may have a brilliant mind, but how is your relationship with your body? You may have a strong athletic body, but how comfortable are you with your feelings and emotions? You may be gifted at work, but how successful are you at home in your intimate relationships? When we cultivate success in a limited arena of our life, like Walter, we may soon realize that something important is missing.

As Mark and I continued our investigation, we discovered another disconcerting pattern. *Our underdeveloped aspects have the power to undermine our overall success and well-being.* I met a brilliant computer programmer who ignored his mental health to the point where he got so depressed, he could no longer work. I interviewed a gifted surgeon who lost his marriage and his hospital contract due to his explosive temper. A beloved teacher lost her job over her addiction to alcohol. A talented business manager was fired for sexually harassing his staff. Mark and I began to see that there were many "successful" people who were being undone by their personal struggles. We wondered...was it possible to create an overall successful life? If so, what would that look like?

As we continued interviewing people, we identified seven areas where people were flourishing or floundering in their personal expression. We came to call these areas the Seven Domains—physical, psychological, cognitive, emotional, relational, spiritual, and integrative aspects that drive our overall functioning. A lack of health or well-being in any one of these areas could directly impact our capacity to be healthy and truly successful.

The Seven Domains are the building blocks that make up every human being, allowing us to create enjoyable, satisfying, meaningful lives.

- *The Psychological Domain* governs our mental health. It is where we make meanings about ourselves and the world, forming the beliefs that steer our life. Our inner narratives and beliefs shape our personality, our behavior, and our outlook on the world.

- *The Physical Domain* involves our body, movement, exercise, and health. It is also the domain where we experience touch, snuggling, sex, and the sense of safety or violation with regard to our body.

- *The Cognitive Domain* refers to our capacity for analytical thinking, reasoning, and organizing. This is where we manage data and information through mental processing.

- *The Emotional Domain* is the realm of our feelings and moods. Because our mind and body are interconnected, we often experience our emotions as both feelings and sensations. For example, when we are sad, we may experience that our "heart hurts." When we are nervous, we may feel sick to our stomach.

- *The Social-Relational Domain* deals with our capacity for connection, emotional intimacy, and social engagement with our partners, family, community, and at work.

- *The Spiritual Domain* encompasses our beliefs and experiences about Divinity and the nature of the Universe. This is where we make sense of reality beyond our material world and our daily human perceptions.

- *The Integrative Domain* is where all our domains synthesize to express the totality of who we are. When all our domains are healthy and vibrant, their integration creates a truly successful life. When our domains are unbalanced—some healthy, some not—our integration reflects the truth of this reality.

The envisioning of the Seven Domains has come from years of working closely with clients and students, listening and learning from their struggles, discerning which aspects of their life were thriving and which aspects were breaking down. Over time, we came to realize that everyone is expressing different levels of domain functioning. In what we call *Lines of Development*, we are well developed in some domains, and less developed in others. This explains why "successful people" can struggle in life. Walter was brilliant in his Cognitive and Physical Domains, but he was less developed in his Emotional and Relational Domains. As his son exclaimed, "You're not going to use me like you use everyone else!"

As you reflect on your life, in which domains do you thrive? In which ones do you struggle? As you aim for a successful life, can you recognize the impact that these domains have on your personal success? What might your life look like if all your domains were equally healthy?

We are all born with certain talents and inclinations. If you are like most people, you probably spend much of your time living in and cultivating the domains you are good at, while avoiding the ones you struggle in. For instance, if you are keenly developed in the Cognitive Domain, you may work as a teacher and spend your free time reading books for pleasure. If you are a computer programmer, you may come home from work and jump on your favorite computer game for relaxation. If you are gifted in the physical domain, you may work as a builder and then spend your weekends hiking or mountain biking. We tend to favor the domains where we experience easy success and satisfaction, which in turn deepens their brilliance and capacity. Do you find this to be true? Do you tend to spend a lot of time "playing" in the domains you're good at?

In the domains where we struggle, we often find barriers and a lack of cultivation. For example, if you contend with a physical disability, you may avoid physical activities. If you struggle with dyslexia, you may shun reading. Our lack of cultivation in various domains can also stem from a deprivation of environmental support. For instance, you may have wanted to be a scientist but grew up in a family that didn't value education. Or you may have wanted to be an athlete, but your family looked down on physical prowess—instead, they pushed you into music or educational pursuits. Other times, we lack cultivation because our communities are under-resourced—there are no libraries or opportunities for education or coaching, or there are no fields to play in. Imagine if Michael Phelps or Katie Ledecky hadn't lived near a pool and received swim lessons; could they have become Olympic swimmers?

At other times, our domains can be hindered by trauma. If you have experienced abuse or suffered injury or illness, you may struggle across your domains. For example, if you have been in a car accident, physically, you may brace every time you get into a car or whenever a car approaches too close. After the accident, you may feel emotionally numb, or your feelings may be volatile and unpredictable. Socially, you may avoid people, believing that others could never understand what you are going through. Spiritually, you may blame God for your misfortune or feel abandoned by the Divine. In any domain that has been touched by trauma, there will be hesitancy, confusion, anxiety, and a tendency to avoid engagement with that domain as we attempt to protect ourselves. Fortunately, it is possible to heal our trauma so we can return to full, vibrant living in all our domains.

* * *

As Mark and I explored what makes a truly successful life, we began to envision what might be possible if humanity were sufficiently cultivated in all Seven Domains. To be clear, we are not advocating domain perfection but rather a level of competence that would allow us to live joyfully in all areas of our life. As humans, we are not meant to thrive in only one or two areas, but across *all* aspects of our existence. With strong, healthy domains, we have the best chance of creating the "fuller life" that Walter and the others were advocating.

While you may have had less than optimal conditions for your development, it is possible to begin cultivating your domains right now. Throughout this book, you will find practices that can help you express yourself more fully in each of the domains. As you engage in these practices, you'll discover more freedom and joy as you release the barriers that have held you back in life. You'll feel refreshed and energized, ready to take up the new learning and growth that can help you realize your dreams. Empowered by your discoveries, you'll embrace a brighter, more authentic expression of yourself—your True Nature—who you are when you are embodying your vitality and inner wisdom, living out the fullness of your passions and potential.

Through our explorations, Mark and I encountered a deeper understanding of success, one beyond external accomplishments. We came to see that no particular achievement, role, or skill guarantees a successful life. True Success doesn't point to material gain, but to a *way of being* that engenders aliveness, authenticity, freedom, and joy, empowering us to live fully in our mind, body, and heart. It is not what we accomplish, but how deeply we embody all our domains that determines our satisfaction, joy, and well-being. When we are expressing our True Nature, we can't help but create a truly successful life.

Interestingly, throughout our interview process, we found that those who felt "truly successful" often reported feeling *blessed* and *satisfied* as a measure of their success. What were they pointing to? Could this experience be made available to everyone, regardless of their external conditions? If so, what kind of cultivation were we aiming for? Our explorations ultimately revealed an inner capacity that not only surprised us, but transformed us personally.

The Seven Domains

The Seven Domains are the building blocks that make up every human being, allowing us to live and create meaningful lives.

- *The Psychological Domain* governs our mental health. It is where we make meanings about ourselves and the world, forming the beliefs that steer our life. Our inner narratives and beliefs shape our personality, our behavior, and our outlook on the world.

- *The Physical Domain* involves our body, movement, exercise, and health. It is also the domain where we experience touch, snuggling, sex, and the sense of safety or violation with regard to our body.

- *The Cognitive Domain* refers to our capacity for analytical thinking, reasoning and organizing. This is where we manage data and information through mental processing.

- *The Emotional Domain* is the realm of our feelings and moods. Because our mind and body are connected, we often experience our emotions as both feelings and sensations. When we are sad, we may experience that our "heart hurts." When we are nervous, we may feel sick to our stomach.

- *The Relational Domain* deals with our capacity for connection, emotional intimacy, and social engagement with our partners, family, community, and at work.

- *The Spiritual Domain* encompasses our beliefs and experiences concerning Divinity and the nature of the Universe. This is where we make sense of the greater reality beyond our material world and our daily human perceptions.

- *The Integrative Domain* is where our domains synthesize together to express the totality of who we are. When our domains are healthy and vibrant, the integration of these capacities creates a truly successful life. When our domains are unbalanced—some healthy, some not—our integration reflects the truth of that reality.

The Markers of True Success

"I'm not sure if this is the right place for me, but my sister thinks you can help." Ryan dropped onto my office couch, throwing me a sweet, boyish smile. "She's been in therapy for a couple of years, so she should know!" Ryan was handsome, well-built, and charming, and I found myself smiling at his easygoing manner. "So, what brings you here?"

"I've been freaking out about work and not sleeping much, and I've got to be on my game."

"And that game would be…"

Ryan told me that he was a wilderness guide. He spent his days guiding backpacking trips, running rafts down rivers, and training people how to rock climb. Listening to his excitement and confidence as he talked, I imagined that he was great at his job, and he found a lot of satisfaction in it. But something must have been "off" in his life; otherwise, he wouldn't have found his way into my office.

"I love running the trips! The problem is Steve—my boss—he's pressuring me to become the general manager. He keeps telling me that he sees 'potential' in me." He rolled his eyes dismissively. "What he's really looking for is someone to take over when he retires. He told me that he thinks of me as a "son" and that my management skills on the trips and with the crews makes me 'perfect' for the job. But I see all the other stuff he does; tons of paperwork, budgets, and contracts..." Ryan's cool demeanor took a sharp turn towards anxiety. "Don't get me wrong, I would love to manage Mountains and Rivers..." His leg started bouncing frenetically. "I really 'get' people, and I have tons of ideas on how to expand the company. So, I should take it, right?" He was squirming in his seat now. "I mean, I'm not getting any younger, and my body's already showing wear and tear. I can't do this physical thing forever."

I smiled kindly. "It sounds like you'd like to take the job. So, what's the problem?"

A flash of fear darkened his face. "I don't know...I don't think I can handle the paperwork—all the budgets, contracts, and scheduling. I'm just not good at that stuff. I'm great with rafting, climbing, and the people...but I *hate* paperwork. And anything having to do with math..." He shuddered. "Whenever I think about it, I get sick to my stomach. If I take the position, everyone's going to find out that I'm not the 'wonder boy' they think I am. It's all going to go to shit, and they'll realize what I really am..."

"An amazing guide and all-around good guy?"

Ryan chuckled in spite of himself. "No. I was thinking, more along the lines of *loser*."

Ryan was bumping up against a struggle many of us face when life changes course or new opportunities emerge. When we get pushed out of our comfort zone, it's easy to collapse into worries, believing that we don't have what it takes to move forward. Ryan desperately wanted to accept the promotion, but he was shackled by fears of not being "smart enough." His beliefs had him convinced that, deep down, he was a "loser," and these beliefs were holding him back from stepping into a new phase of his life, one that he felt called to.

Engaging Your Limiting Stories

What inner stories are keeping you from living fully? Perhaps you carry some fearful stories or imagine that bad things will happen if you pursue your passions. Maybe you believe that someone you care about will be upset if you follow your aspirations. Or perhaps you hold a great regret that weighs heavily on you, and you believe that you don't deserve to be happy...in a loving relationship...or allowed to follow the passions that would fulfill your soul.

Who would you be without these stories? I invite you to take a moment and imagine your life free of these dictates. What choices can you make now? Can you take a step in that direction?

To help Ryan understand his predicament and soften his self-judgment, in our next session I introduced Ryan to the Seven Domains, explaining the faculties that each domain holds, detailing how we can be strong in certain areas, while we struggle in others. "Ryan, you're really well-developed in your Physical Domain, but you're struggling in the Cognitive Domain. Anytime we ignore our underdeveloped aspects, they tend to disrupt our life—they can compromise our overall success, or they can keep us from living the life we're called to. It sounds like you're flourishing as a wilderness guide, but your fears about your cognitive issues are keeping you from stepping into a job that you're really interested in."

Ryan nodded thoughtfully. "I like this domain thing. It makes a lot of sense. I know this one guy who's an amazing guide, but he lost his job because he started drinking too much—he was showing up to work drunk."

I nodded. "Those kinds of breakdowns happen all the time. We can be incredibly gifted in one area, creating lots of success, yet our underdeveloped aspects can definitely take us down. In order to be truly successful, we want to attend to all our domains, so they're all healthy and flourishing."

To bring home the point, I handed Ryan a graph sheet with the Seven Domains coupled with a four-point scale to assess his level of functioning in each area. "If you take a moment to do this assessment, it will give you a 'big picture' overview of how you're functioning in life; you'll see which areas are well developed and which one need more attention. When you can see your capacities clearly, you can begin attending to the domains that are holding you back. Once you cultivate these areas, I think you'll be able to step into the life that's calling to you."

"You sound like my sister," Ryan said with a grin. Holding up the paper, he read aloud:

- **Gifted:** Our functioning in the domain is exceptional, beyond what is considered typical for our age or development.
- **Competent:** Our functioning is considered "normal" for our development and culture.
- **Challenged:** We have significant difficulty in the domain, or we are floundering.
- **Mixed:** Development is normal in some parts of the domain, while challenged in others. (i.e., it's possible to be cognitively brilliant yet contend with a learning deficit.)

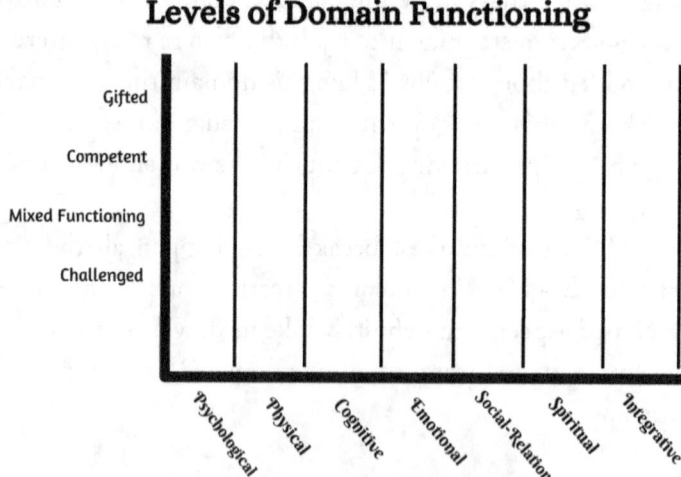

Levels of Domain Functioning

Gifted

Competent

Mixed Functioning

Challenged

Psychological   Physical   Cognitive   Emotional   Social-Relational   Spiritual   Integrative

"Okay, I get this," he said, reaching for a pen. Psychological Domain… What do you mean by 'the meanings and stories that guide our life'?"

"Well, as we go through life encountering different experiences, we tell ourselves stories and narratives to help us make sense of these events. For example, imagine that a kid strikes out in baseball, and everyone laughs at them. In the heat of their embarrassment and humiliation, they may tell themselves, *Baseball is stupid!* If they come to believe that 'baseball is stupid,' they may give up entirely on baseball and never play again and their belief and withdrawal from the game would guarantee that the child never develops their baseball skills. Worse yet, they may walk away from all sports. However, if that same child strikes out and everyone is supportive and encouraging, helping them to release their humiliation, they may decide that baseball is still a great game. They might tell themselves, *I just have to practice harder, then I'll be a great ballplayer!* That belief will lead to more positive experiences in sports."

"Our psychology is a reflection of our mind-states, attitudes and beliefs, which in turn shape our thoughts, behavior and outlook on life. For instance, if we believe that people are 'good' and 'kind,' we'll greet the world with a friendly smile. But if we believe that people are 'mean' and 'no one can be trusted,' we'll see the world as threatening and act accordingly. And if our stories don't line up with reality, for instance, if we believe that everyone is an alien, we struggle even more; that's when we're dealing with mental illness. As I reflect on your stories, they seem aligned with reality, and your narratives—particularly around guiding and being outdoors— are pretty enlivening and playful. Overall, you seem happy and content."

Ryan smiled. "I guess I do carry a lot of happy beliefs, but I don't ever *think* about beliefs or their meanings. I'm more of a live-in-the-moment kind of guy."

"So you're psychologically healthy, but you wouldn't say you're psychologically 'aware' of your stories and beliefs, understanding what is driving you deep down inside."

Ryan nodded. "Yeah, that captures it. So, should I put that down as 'competent?' That sounds good to me!"

A little more thoughtful now, Ryan continued reading the list. "Physical Domain... Alright, I'm a raft guide, I ski, I backpack... so I think that qualifies me as 'gifted' in the Physical Domain. Cognitive... Yeah, I don't do so well there. Math and reading have always been hard for me. So, I'll put that down as 'challenged.'"

"Okay, the Emotional domain... Yeah, I don't think about emotions either... But I think I have pretty healthy emotions. I'm not like my friend Jeff; he loses his temper all the time. And my sister says I'm 'emotionally intelligent'—whatever that means. But she should know! I'll put that down as 'competent.' Social-Relational Domain..." Ryan smiled brightly. "Oh, I'm great at this one! I get along with *everybody*, and I do okay on dating!" He grinned. "I'm going to mark that as 'gifted.' Now, the Spiritual Domain... I don't go to church, but I've always felt nature is my church. Running rivers is a spiritual thing. You know what, I'm going to put that down as 'gifted.' And the Integrative Domain... What's that again?"

"The Integrative Domain is where the intelligence and strengths of our domains fuse together to express who we are in a given moment. If we're struggling in any domains, our integration will reflect that—we can only be as healthy and successful as our domains are. When our domains are strong and balanced, our integration looks strong and vibrant, and we live fully in everything we do."

"That's what happens when I'm on the river! I get into this 'flow state.' It's amazing when that happens!"

I smiled. "Exactly! In those moments, everything comes together, and our integration reflects what I like to call our 'True Nature.'"

He grinned. "When I'm outdoors, I'm definitely in my True Nature." He paused, suddenly looking sober. "But then there's that math and reading thing. When I'm dealing with that, I don't feel integrated at all. Maybe I should put this one down as 'mixed.'"

Ryan held up his sheet, amazed. "Look at this... It looks like a roller coaster! I'm up, I'm down... If my Cognitive and Integrative Domains were as high as Physical and Spiritual, I'd be amazing! Look at this!" He handed me his checklist.

As I looked over his graph, I wasn't surprised. Most of us start out with this kind of profile—we're amazing in some areas and struggle in others. As I explained to Ryan, this is totally normal. Handing him back the graph, I got straight to the point: "So, being a general manager involves lots of reports and budgets. And reports and budgets involve math and reading."

Ryan blanched. "Yeah, don't remind me." He sighed, disheartened. "I'm no good at that stuff... Maybe I should just forget it. I can't do this job. I don't know what I was thinking."

"Hold on," I said smiling. "The whole reason we do a domain assessment is to get an accurate look at our functioning. Looking over your graph, it's clear that you're not a *loser*." He smiled sheepishly, remembering his self-disparaging remark. "Yet you do have some issues with math and reading. If you attend to your blocks in these areas, I bet you can find a path to becoming a manager. That's what you want, right?"

Ryan smiled, not entirely bought into the idea. "Yeah, I want the job... But I haven't touched math in years. I've kinda worked my life so I could avoid it."

I nodded, sympathetically. "And that's the problem. If we avoid our difficult domains, we can't develop them. So, are you willing to give it a try?"

Ryan nodded reluctantly. "Sure. My sister's already designed a manager's shirt for me. She's convinced I'm going to be the manager." He grinned. "It'd be a shame to let her down."

I smiled back. "It sounds like she's got your back."

Ryan chuckled. "She does!" We went ahead and set up a time to meet the following week, agreeing to take a deeper look at his Cognitive Domain.

Laying the Foundation for True Success

Like so many of my clients, Ryan came to therapy asking me to fix something that he thought was broken. He thought if he knew how to *do* something better, he might *be* someone better and that would bring him happiness and fulfillment. But as we would discover, he was putting the cart before the horse. As Mark and I continued our investigation, we began to notice that truly successful people embodied certain qualities and characteristics that made them feel happy and fulfilled, whether or not they possess money, status, or the standard measures of success lauded by our society. Furthermore, these qualities or *ways of being* engendered certain behaviors that actualized successful outcomes, giving rise to a more successful life.

This realization came into sharp relief during a workshop Mark and I facilitated at a local school. As part of our community work, Mark and I regularly provide consultations and trainings to various groups and organizations, so we were happy to oblige when a middle school principal invited us to offer a daylong training to his staff, as they were looking for new ways to address academic failure in the classroom. Rather than offer the usual behavioral interventions, Mark and I wanted to suggest a new framework for what it means to be successful, convinced that this would not only make a positive difference in the classroom, but in the lives of their students.

On the day of the training, we watched as the teachers and staff filed into the auditorium. Many of them looked stressed and exhausted and a few looked downright irritated to be there. This didn't surprise us. In our consulting, we had seen that teachers are often overworked, under-resourced, and besieged with new training programs as schools aim to satisfy their funding and licensing requirements. Wishing to offset the displeasure of sitting through yet one more training, we had brought coffee and breakfast treats to offer a little nourishment.

When everyone was settled with something warm and tasty, we opened the day with an inquiry: "What makes your job difficult?" The teachers looked surprised. They are rarely asked about the *real* issues they face in their classrooms. They seemed eager to respond, shooting off their answers rapidly and to the point:

"Interruptions... conflicts between kids... lack of motivation... no group skills... emotional neediness... attendance issues... disrespect... distractibility... health issues... impulsiveness... anger... violence... depression... home difficulties... mental health issues..."

Mark wrote the answers on the board. Here was a clear definition of the problem. When he was done writing, Mark turned to face the group, opening the topic of the day.

"Thanks for your answers. Now I want to ask you, *what is true success?*"

The room fell silent. Puzzled faces looked to each other as the teachers glanced around, wondering who might have an answer. As the silence continued, we sensed an edginess and discomfort rising in the group. With a tone of irritation, one teacher asked, "Are you talking about success with money or professionally?" Another spoke, with an air of annoyance: "Do you mean fame and power, or are you talking about success in education?" Looking at the disgruntled faces we could see that some of them were beginning to wonder if this workshop might be a waste of their time. Clearly, we were not offering the tools they expected for managing a classroom.

To quell the tension, I rephrased the question. "Let's make it personal. What does living a truly successful life mean to you?" Again, the first responses were testy. "It depends... It's relative... It's subjective..."

What is true success? We have asked hundreds of people this question and consistently we get the same response. Initially, people pause and there seems to be some confusion, along with a sense of tension. For many, the problem lies with the word *success*. Some snap back, "Success makes me think of business, and we're talking about my life!" This idea—that success is linked to business—is one of the ideas we want to challenge. What might be possible if we reimagine the word "success" as a marker of personal health and well-being rather than an index of prosperity?

Other times, tensions arise with the phrase "true success." This modifier seems to raise the stakes, making many people defensive. We often hear, "My success is *true* success! What are you implying?!" The word, "true" seems to challenge the validity of our success. Perhaps we may fear that, as Walter found, that we have been "barking up the wrong tree" our whole life. What if our success isn't *true* success? These issues are in fact what we intend to highlight in asking this question. Sometimes, the only way to realize true success is to explore what it isn't.

As the workshop progressed, the teachers were struggling to find an answer. One ventured, "It's having enough money and things. No wait! It's having respect and living within your values." Another added, "Yeah, but you have to have enough money to care for your family." Another quietly suggested, "It's being honest and devoting your life to God." They went around and around, their initial answers bouncing between amassing wealth and living ethically. The confusion and uncertainty were palpable in the room.

Then, in a single moment, the tide turned. Thoughtfully, one teacher offered, "Okay, true success can't be about money. My uncle is truly successful, and he doesn't have any money. He works with drug abusers, helping them get clean."

An administrator chimed in, "It can't be about fame. I know plenty of people whom I consider truly successful, and they aren't famous."

"Could it be about personal power?" offered another teacher. "You need to make your life go in a certain direction."

Another teacher countered, "But you have to be careful with power. I can think of lots of people who have power, and I wouldn't consider them successful."

The group was warming up, playing off each other's ideas, tapping into an intuitive wisdom, naming traits that lay beyond our accustomed notions of success. Soon the answers were coming as fast as when they'd named their challenges: "You have to have good people skills… Communication skills… Know how to handle problems… Care about people… Be disciplined… Have integrity… Resist peer pressure… Know what you want… Know what's really important in life…"

As they called out their answers, Mark wrote this new list on the board. When they finished, the room felt lighter, more joyful. People were smiling and they looked refreshed. Here, written out before them was a new paradigm, a new way of conceiving of success. If our standard measure of success included these qualities, teachers and students alike would be successful both in the classroom and out in the world. This measure of success was not limited to perfect grades or other attainments, but extended to something much deeper, accessing the potential of every student.

The traits named by the teachers that engender True Success included:

Self-Awareness

Sees the Big Picture

Self-Motivated

Disciplined/Determined

Emotionally Intelligent

Works Well with Others

Seeks to Understand

Lifelong Learner

Respectful and Respected

Is a Good Listener

Follows and Develops their Passions

Sets Goals and Follows Through

Displays Clear and Flexible Thinking

Cares About and Helps Others

Knows How to Manage Stress

Gives Back to their Community

Is Resilient

Helps Others Shine

Has Integrity

Is Creative

> What happens to your idea of "success" when it shifts from something to attain to *a way of being*?

As you read through this list, how do you feel? Can you sense a certain lightness and potential? What happens to your idea of "success" when it shifts from something to attain to *a way of being*? As we reviewed these traits with the teachers that day, I found myself smiling and relaxing. Imagining these qualities opened a sense of trust and ease in me, and I knew that any person possessing these attributes would do well in life. Mark and I have come to call these attributes the *Success Traits*. These are the qualities of truly successful people *and* they promote success in all Seven Domains.

Interestingly, many of the qualities identified by the teachers that day were the same ones cited by Mark's patients when they'd dreamed of a second chance at life. They'd told Mark that given the chance, they would be more loving, more accountable, more authentic. They would care for their family and their community. They would live with integrity and cultivate their inner strength to stand up to those who pressured them to abandon their truth, passions, and dreams. Every time Mark and I present this exercise, the same Success Traits appear again and again. It is as if some greater wisdom lies within us, waiting for the right question or circumstances to open the door to this intelligence. Remarkably, money, fame, power, and winning, while often brought up early in the process, never make the final list.

> *Look closely at the present you are constructing:*
> *It should look like the future you are dreaming.*
> *— Alice Walker*

To be clear, there is nothing inherently wrong with money, fame, power, or winning. A truly successful person may have any or all of these, especially when they arise out of fulfilling our passions. For instance, if you love acting and you are gifted at it, you may have a wonderful career that includes plenty of fame and money. But a great actor may not be living a truly successful life if they are struggling in other domains—for example, if they are addicted to drugs and alcohol. A truly successful actor would embody the Success Traits both in their acting career and in their personal life.

We might ask, are the qualities that the teachers named that day innate or are they cultivated? As with many things, it's a case of nature and nurture. We are born with a capacity to *be self-aware, care for others, be lifelong learners,* etc., but it is through our conditioning that these capacities develop or atrophy. The Success Traits are not qualities of "special people;" they are expressions of our potential as human beings. They arise from an inspired place within all of us that is connected to our integrity, strength, and deeper intelligence. When we are connected to this inner intelligence, we awaken to the fullness of who we are. This inner resource and the Success Traits that arise out of it embodies the foundation of True Success.

> The Success Traits are not qualities of "special people;" they are expressions of our potential as human beings.

Shooting the Rapids

The next time I saw Ryan, he trudged into the office and flopped dramatically onto the couch. "So, how do we fix this *cognitive* stuff?" The way he said 'cognitive' made it sound like it left a bad taste in his mouth.

I smiled. "It sounds like you're ready to work!"

He threw me a pouty frown. "No, I'm *ready* to stop feeling nauseous every time I think about the manager's job."

I smiled, happy that he was willing to jump in. "Okay, let's start with a practice that can help you get calm and focused. That way, when we work on the math and reading stuff, you won't become anxious or nauseous. These skills I'm going to show you will also help you be successful should you decide to take the manager position."

Ryan sat up straighter, "You think that's possible? You can help me do that?"

"Actually, *you* can do that! You know that part of you that holds the boat when you're shooting through the rapids with a raft full of screaming tourists?"

Ryan grinned. "Yeah! I love it! It's the best feeling in the world! I feel strong... I'm flowing with the river... It's an incredible feeling!"

"Exactly! And is it possible for you to still have that feeling, even when you don't know what's coming, or there's a big change in the water?"

Ryan smiled confidently. "Sure! When you're in 'the zone' there's no problem! You just feel the water, ride the energy...and this 'sweet spot' opens. I don't know what to call it, but it always carries you through. You don't even have to think... You just trust it and flow with it."

I smiled. "Well, that *deeper part of you* is what we're going to access today."

Ryan threw me a sideward glance. "Yeah... but that only happens on the river, or when I'm outdoors."

"Actually, you can access that part of you anytime. And when you're in touch with it, you can handle anything—on the river *and* in life. Let me show you how to get in touch with it. It is a source of strength and well-being, and when you're connected with it, you'll be able to handle your 'cognitive stuff.' Are you up for giving it a try?" I offered him a reassuring smile. Smiling back, he looked like an excited boy. "Sure!"

The Essence of Success

As Mark and I reflected on the Success Traits, it was clear that these traits were more than just skills to be developed—they were inner qualities to be accessed. But how could we unlock these attributes? What was the *source* of this goodness, caring, compassion, and wisdom expressing as the Success Traits? Could we teach others how to open these traits in a consistent manner that they could rely on? The answer came when I encountered the wellspring of this goodness—a source that changed our life, our marriage, and our approach to creating success.

One warm summer evening, Mark and I hosted a dinner party for a few of our friends. As we sat outside sharing appetizers and stories, the conversation wound its way to our work, and Mark and I excitedly shared our discovery of the Success Traits. Over dinner we debated about the nature of the Success Traits—some of our friends argued that they were skills to be developed, while others argued that they must be innate. Never reaching a clear consensus, everyone went home, and Mark and I were left to contemplate the mystery. Reflecting on the traits, it seemed clear to us that these qualities were products of *nature* and *nurture*—that they were part of our nature, but they had to be cultivated. But where did they originate from? We felt close to an understanding, but we couldn't quite put our finger on it.

Finishing the dishes, Mark headed off to bed as he had to be at work early the next day. Being a night owl, I still felt wide awake, so I decided to do a meditation. I sat quietly on the couch, breathing out my tension, and I let go of my day.

When I opened my eyes, I felt refreshed and relaxed. Glancing down, I noticed a copy of the Success Traits sitting on the coffee table. I reached over and picked it up, quietly reading through the qualities. There was something familiar about the qualities...they inspired an inner tone of strength, resilience, and confidence, and as I read each one, I felt a calmful joy arising in me. What was the *source* of these feelings? Where was this calm and joy coming from?

I decided to do a little experiment. I got up and began walking around the room, embodying each trait. Being "self-aware," I found myself walking taller with a sense of presence and deep connection to myself. I felt oriented to my whole being, no longer absorbed in my mind, the way I usually am. When I tried on "respected and respectful," I felt safe, as if I was protected by a field of positive regard. "Seeking to understand" brought a feeling of curiosity and a willingness to engage, not my usual bracing against the unfamiliar. "Being creative," I was flooded with imaginative impulses and felt confidence and delight in the prospect of expressing my creative ideas.

There was something familiar about every quality I tried on, as if they were part of my deeper nature. As I continued to feel their expressions arising within me, I noticed that they seemed to emanate from the *center* of me. It wasn't exactly where my heart was, but instead a space in the center of my being. I turned my attention to this space and began breathing into it, allowing myself to become fully present with it. Resting in this presence, I was awash in deep peace, feeling as if I were sensing my true self—the "real me" underneath all the stories and beliefs that make up who I consider "Maureen" to be. In touch with the *essence* of me, I was connected to something pure and basic, beyond my usual fears, stories, and cultural conditioning. Feeling at home within myself—whole, centered, calm, and complete—I sensed that this "essence" could meet everything with grace, wisdom, and effectiveness, no matter what "Maureen" was experiencing.

As I continued to focus on this essence, I began to notice that it had a certain dynamic aliveness. Sometimes, I could feel it softly vibrating. Other times, it moved with the rhythm of my breath, soothing and comforting. After some time, I could sense it rising into form, coalescing into thoughts, feelings, and sensations, and in that moment, I realized that I was witnessing my Lifeforce responding to life.

In touch with my essence, I felt happy, content, and utterly free. I was free to be myself, to live joyfully, and express my passions. I felt no fear; there was just calm, piercing clarity. I knew what truly mattered to me and I felt empowered to express my beliefs and passions. I also understood that this essence was a source of great integrity, so I could trust myself to live authentically and genuinely, unencumbered by the expectations or judgments of others. The more I opened to its peace and ease, the happier and more playful I felt. At one point, I felt so free I began laughing and dancing around the room, smiling in ecstasy in a freedom I had not felt since childhood.

I don't know how long I reveled in that freedom and ecstasy, but I remember that my jaw hurt from smiling so much. After some time, the energy settled, and I lay on the floor to rest, peaceful, spacious, and open. As I lay quietly, my mind drifted, and I found myself reflecting on family, friends, and beloved mentors, filled with joy and gratitude for their presence and love in my life. Suddenly, out of nowhere, the gratitude swelled into a great rush of love—not only for the people in my life, but for everyone, everywhere. I was so filled with love that I began laughing and crying at the same time, and in that love, there was only one longing: That everyone could experience the peace, joy, safety, and contentment of what I would now call, *Essence*.

Engaging Your Success Traits

I invite you to find a moment when you can be quiet and alone—maybe early in the morning, late at night, or while out in nature. Look over the list of Success Traits, letting yourself feel into and embody each one. Where in your body do you experience each quality arising? Allow yourself to rest in the space where these qualities are emerging. Breathe into this space, expanding into the fullness of your Essence, feeling its peace, joy, and compassion arise in you. Imagine this as a normal, ordinary experience.

Discovering Essence changed my life. Before I encountered Essence, I lived with a fear that I wasn't really "good enough." Believing that I was somehow broken, I had always been working to improve myself, trying to achieve something that would help me transcend my inferiority and brokenness. This identity—that I was a broken person in need of improvement—is what I came to call, "Maureen Incorporated" or "Me Inc." a fictional self that obscured my deeper Essence. In discovering Essence, I experienced that deep at my core I am an inherently good person—my essential nature is kind, caring, and loving. With Essence, I came home to who I had been as a small child, before all the pain in life had shut me down. I was now simply "Maureen" and in touch with my true foundation. I knew I could trust myself to live well, be authentic, and realize my potential. Pierced with clarity, I understood Essence to be the wellspring of the Success Traits. Essence was the source of the qualities Walter and the teachers were pointing to. If I could embody Essence and help others locate their Essence, they could discover the qualities that could bring them True Success.

What is Essence?

The dictionary defines *essence* as "the real or ultimate nature of a thing; the most significant quality or aspect of a thing or person." Over the years I have heard people refer to Essence by many names: *Peace, Stillness, Heart, Soul, Presence, Logos, Silence, The Witness, the Quiet within, Awareness, Wisdom, Buddha Nature, our Natural Mind, our Deep Unconscious, True Beingness,* and *Love.* In the Aboriginal culture of Australia, the deep inner listening of *Dadirri* points to Essence. In mystical Christianity, it might be likened to the concept of Christ Consciousness or the Sacred Heart. Like facets of a diamond, each of these terms reveals its qualities of peace, transcendence, love, and wisdom, experienced by people all across the world at different times and in different places. If we take time to sit in Essence, we may easily recognize its qualities in each of these descriptions.

As you discover this deeper part of yourself, I invite you to use whatever word captures your experience. If "Essence" brings up resistance, see if there is another word that resonates more deeply with you. You may prefer *contentment, ease, aliveness,* or one of the words above. If you choose a different term, I invite you to substitute your word anytime you see "Essence" in the book.

All of us have touched Essence. We may feel its presence when we dance, write, run, play music, or lovingly tend our garden, swept up in the flow and intimacy of our acts. Anytime we are "in the zone" we open to its inner stillness and presence: Focused and flowing, we are present-moment oriented—our actions are spontaneously creative, seemingly effortless, and filled with delight and fulfillment. We may also experience Essence in moments when our mind is caught off guard. Walking along, we may be chattering to ourselves, when we turn a corner and encounter a beautiful sunset. Undone by the beauty before us, our thinking stops as we are absorbed in awe. In that "silence," we feel whole, complete, and deeply nourished. For a moment, we are *home*—we need for nothing, we are free of our history, and we are simply *being,* enjoying the bliss of our inner peace and the beauty of this world. In these moments, we are embodied in our True Nature.

When I am in touch with Essence, I love feeling its dynamic qualities. As I sit mindfully, I feel its energy moving much like the rise and fall of ocean swells or the gentle rocking of a boat on a lake. If I see a suffering person or animal, I feel its energy rise up as compassion. When I see a beloved person or pet, I feel it rise in friendliness, joy, and love. Its response to the world is always kind, wise, and informed for it sees everyone and everything with clear, compassionate eyes. Since it is not entangled with the fears and conditioning of "Maureen Inc.," it expresses my true heart, my integrity, and my passions, paving the way to a truly successful life.

Once we become familiar with the qualities of Essence, we begin to recognize its presence everywhere. Our brother or sister may describe a moment of being in "the zone" as they exercise, and we smile, familiar with their description of Essence. We may hear Essence expressed by elders as they speak about the beauty and simplicity of the "good old days." We may see Essence expressed in the eyes of a loved one as they surrender to their last days of life, Essence smiling at us from their softening face. Or we might be pierced by Essence while contemplating art, while dancing, drumming, singing at church, praying to the Divine, or listening to the laughter of children as they run through a park.

Children are always bubbling with Essence for they haven't closed off to it. They embody Essence while running, laughing, in the loving looks they give to us, and in the small acts of kindness they offer us. When we are connected with our own Essence, we have an opportunity to meet children in the "love zone." We might share an exchange of love and joy as we look into their sparkling eyes, we may get swept up in the pleasure of looking at pretty rocks with them, or our heart leaps with joy, seeing the beauty of the flowers they picked. In Essence, we see the world as children see it, filled with the joy, freedom, and intimacy of an open, loving heart.

The more I embrace Essence, the more I see it mirrored in the world. I hear it reflected in the poetry and wisdom teachings of the East—in Kabir, Mirabai, Rumi, Confucius, the Buddha, and in the compassion teachings of Christianity and Judaism. I feel its presence in the works of poets and artists from the West—Walt Whitman, Georgia O'Keefe,

Vincent van Gogh, Mark Rothko, Alice Walker, and T.S. Eliot. It is found in the great works of science—you can hear it reflected in Einstein's musings, Richard Feynman's quantum descriptions, and Neil deGrasse Tyson's passion as he describes the Cosmos. When we look to the icons who express Essence in their work, all of them describe some form of turning inward or resting in Silence or Stillness. They may reference Essence by different names, but it is possible to hear its qualities reflected in their offerings.

> *We shall not cease from exploration, and the end of all our*
> *exploring will be to arrive where we started and know*
> *the place for the first time.*
> —*T. S. Eliot*

Essence is a natural feature of our humanity and yet most of us are never taught how to intentionally connect with it. Sometimes, spontaneous experiences of Essence are even seen as "weird" or frightening. But as you come to know this deeper part of yourself, you will begin to see that it is simply your natural mind—who you are when you are unclouded by fear, pain, and limiting beliefs. The more you rest in your Essence, the more you develop and express your True Nature.

> The more you rest in your Essence, the more you develop and express your True Nature.

Opening To Essence

As Ryan settled into the couch, he looked a bit skeptical. "So, you're saying that the way I feel on the river, I can feel that way in the rest of my life?"

I smiled. "Well, I don't think you'll spend your days in rushing ecstasy, if that's what you mean. When you're on a river trip, does every moment in Essence feel like riding the rapids?"

Ryan shook his head, smiling. "No. Sometimes at the end of the day when I'm sitting on the riverbank watching a sunset or sitting around the campfire, I feel this quiet, peaceful energy in the center of my chest. Sitting by the fire, sometimes I feel love for everything and everyone there."

Smiling, I agreed. "Sometimes this inner energy is quiet, loving, and peaceful. Other times, it can be quite energetic. Its form looks different depending on the situation. But we can learn to recognize this Essence— calm, loving, strong—in any form it takes. Why don't we deepen into it and see how it might support you in this job transition." Ryan nodded, taking a moment to arrange the pillows on the couch. When he was comfortable, I invited him to close his eyes.

"Okay, so as you're sitting with your eyes closed, take a couple of quieting breaths and notice what's happening in your mind, body, or heart right now."

Ryan opened one eye. "This feels weird." He sat up and rubbed his eyes, throwing me a playful grin. "This doesn't feel like when I'm on the river."

I grinned back. "That's because we're not at the river part yet; we've just started! Since we don't have the big outdoors, we need another way to access this deeper, wider part of ourselves. So I'm introducing a bit of mindfulness to help us connect to this soothing presence. Would you be willing to try the practice and see where it lands?" Ryan nodded, but he looked skeptical.

Making sure that he was comfortable, I asked, "Are there any other concerns?" He shook his head, no.

"Okay, then go ahead and close your eyes and take a few clearing breaths, just so you can pay attention to your experience..." He closed his eyes and took a few deep breaths. "Now, just notice what's happening in your body, heart, or mind in this moment. No need to change any of it; just notice what's happening."

He was silent a moment, then he hesitantly said, "There's buzzing energy in my body...and there's a voice saying, 'This is stupid.' I don't think I'm doing it right."

"Actually, that's exactly what we're looking for. So, your body's buzzing with energy and there's a voice commenting...that's perfectly normal. Often, when we begin mindfulness practice, we're very busy inside. Now imagine for a moment, that you can gently breathe out that busyness with each exhale—on each outbreath, you're breathing out the busy energy and the worry that comes with that voice... We're just doing this to 'empty out' some stress and settle a bit." I watched as Ryan's exhales grew longer. After a few minutes, he sank into the cushions and his shoulders relaxed.

"Now, there may still be some busy energy swirling around, but imagine that you can let that energy reside in the *front part* of your body—perhaps in your chest or the front of your torso—and see if you can sense any quiet or peacefulness in the background, deeper inside your body."

A moment later, Ryan nodded. "Wonderful. If you like, imagine that you can 'step back' into that peace, away from the busy energy." I paused. "Are you able to 'step back' into the peace and quiet?" He nodded. "Once you feel the peace, begin breathing into it or 'with' it, letting the peaceful quiet expand and come into focus. You're not trying to *grow* it; you're just allowing it to expand naturally with each breath." I sat silently for a few moments, letting him settle into the ease.

Sensing a deepening happening inside Ryan, I added another step. "If you like, you can let yourself *become* this peace. Let go of any thinking and imagine that the 'Peace' is breathing. You're relaxed, and 'Peace' is breathing quietly." I watched as Ryan relaxed even more deeply. When I sensed that he was deeply anchored in a restful presence, I quietly said, "This peace and ease is what I call Essence, a part of you that is always here, just underneath or 'behind' all the busyness of your usual mind. You might recognize this as the presence you feel when you're on the river."

Ryan nodded. Softly, he said, "Yeah, this is it. But it's bigger on the river. And it doesn't feel like 'essence' to me, it feels more like *Life*."

"You're welcome to refer to it in the way that feels right to you. If you like, you can open to this energy of Life fully, just as you do on the river."

After a few quiet moments, he spoke. "Yeah, this is it... I never knew I could access this on my own. It definitely feels like the energy of Life; it's a Lifeforce."

I sat quietly, giving him the space to enjoy the experience. When the time seemed right, I deepened the exploration. "So, as you're feeling into this Lifeforce, what qualities are you noticing? How is this Lifeforce showing up right now?"

"I feel calm, strong… and 'bigger.'"

I smiled, having heard this description many times. "Wonderful. So, with this sense of calm strength and feeling 'bigger,' imagine yourself as the manager of Mountains and Rivers embodying this strength and centeredness—you're training guides, giving pep talks, managing the day-to-day stuff…and there's some budgeting and paperwork. *Don't think.* Just let your Lifeforce feel into being a manager."

As I waited, I noticed a change in Ryan. With his eyes still closed, he lifted his head and sat up straight, a small smile playing at the corners of his mouth.

Softly, I asked, "Does this Lifeforce have a sense about this job? For example, is the job to 'too much' or too overwhelming for *Life?*"

Ryan shook his head. "No. I feel happy. I feel really comfortable doing all the manager stuff." A soft smile brightened his face. "My Lifeforce wants me to take the job. It knows I can do it."

> *Learn the backward step that turns your light inward*
> *to illuminate yourself.*
> —Dogen

* * *

Why this sudden change in Ryan's experience? What allowed him to suddenly feel happy and at home in the management job? It came from a shift in perspective. When Ryan accessed the "Quiet" deep inside him, opening his "Lifeforce," he shifted his focus from the torment of his inner fears to a deeper part of his being that is not entangled with his history or his conditioning. Like Ryan, we can learn to shift our attention from our anxious stories to the deeper peace within us—it's simply a matter of focus and attention. Our Essence doesn't go away; it is always sitting quietly behind our busy thoughts. When we breathe out our tension and stress, we can see that it is the "Quiet" that remains.

In my workshops, I like to illustrate this stepping back practice with the metaphor of a whiteboard. Imagine that Essence is the clean, shiny whiteboard; it is our natural mind—clear and ever-present. The writing on the board is all the stories we've lived out: Sometimes, happy stories get written on the board; sometimes sad stories or painful stories get written on the board. As time goes on, we become more and more focused on the stories and forget all about the whiteboard—our Essence, our foundation. But behind all these busy stories, the whiteboard is always there, unchanged and unimpacted by the words. For example, if someone wrote on the board, "You're a fat, stupid idiot!" Is the whiteboard affected by these words? Of course not.

When we rediscover our whiteboard, we can see for ourselves that our foundation is alive, well, and healthy, unharmed by the stories and experiences we've lived. It's much like the figure-ground illusion of the goblet and the silhouette of two faces looking at each other: Do you see the faces or the goblet? Once you see both, you can go back and forth. It's possible to train ourselves to feel our Essence again and come back to its clear, peaceful presence anytime we want to live from this wise, peaceful space within us.

Meeting Your Essence

Find a comfortable place to sit and allow your eyes to close or look softly at the floor. Gently breathe out any stress or tension that you are feeling in your body. You can also breathe out racing or stressful thoughts in your mind, or any painful emotions that may be present in your heart.

When you feel more settled, imagine that any remaining busyness, pain, or stress is residing in the *front half* of your body—in your chest or torso—and take a moment to notice any peace or quiet that is resting deeper in the background. You might also notice some area of "comfort" or "warmth" in your body. Once you locate this comfortable, quiet space, imagine that you can breathe into this peace and quiet, letting it expand and come into focus. If you like, you can also play with letting yourself *become* the peace: Imagine yourself as "Peace," "Comfort," or "Warmth" breathing.

Let yourself rest in your Essence.

The process of imagining ourselves *stepping back* to access Essence works well for many, yet there are many other ways to access Essence. Some people prefer to "step left" to shift away from the busyness of their mind. Others prefer to drop into a quiet spaciousness within their body. Some love to breathe into a safe warm space within their body. For others, it's easiest to access Essence in the freedom of movement—running, swimming, or riding their bike. And for some, they simply need to connect with the quiet spaciousness of the room around them, breathing into that open space. As you explore Essence, I invite you to play with these variations to find the method that works best for you.

For some people, it can be a struggle to locate the quiet within, particularly when we are stressed or carry a lot of anxiety. If this is the case for you, I encourage you to be gentle with yourself. You can begin by simply breathing out the tension in your body. As you empty out more stress, you'll begin to settle and notice a "quieting" within; this is the quiet that opens the door to Essence. You might also find it helpful to access Essence with your eyes open—sitting out in nature, relaxing in the safety of your bedroom, or resting on a bench at your favorite park can support a sense of peace and ease that can more readily open the door to sensing your Essence.

As you begin to practice with Essence, if at any time you experience a sense of discomfort or overwhelm, simply open your eyes and look around, bringing yourself back to your present environment. If you experience a lot of anxiety, you might take a moment to name some familiar objects that you see in your environment. It can also feel comforting to look around you or behind you; this can help you relax and add to your sense of safety. You might also take a moment to feel the bottom of your feet on the floor or notice where your legs are making contact with your cushion or chair. Touching into these physical sensations can help us focus our mind, bringing soothing to our mind and body. If you find that you are easily triggered into anxiety or overwhelm, you might consider reaching out for some therapeutic support; it can be greatly helpful as we delve into our healing and self-care.

As you explore Essence, it's important to pace yourself, taking all the time you need to feel safe and comfortable. We can open to Essence at any time in our life, when we are young or old, so there is no rush. Once you are familiar with Essence, it will become a natural refuge, offering you a space of respite in your busy world.

Living Life with Essence

Whenever we are caught up in fears and the stressors of "Me Inc.," a moment of "stepping back" allows us to touch into our deeper nature, assuring us that deep down, we are okay. The more we untangle ourselves from our fears and limitations, the more we open to a sense of wholeness, strength, and integrity that allows us to meet the world differently. As Ryan and I continued our work together, he would come to see that both on the river, and in life, Essence is never overwhelmed. It sits back, viewing the world with a quiet countenance, arousing the wisdom that expresses the Success Traits. With Essence, Ryan would not only move past his challenges in the Cognitive Domain, but he would open his potential *across* his domains. Ryan was on his way to realizing what it means to live a truly successful life, full of satisfaction and inspiration.

To uncover the power of Essence in your own life, you might experiment with opening Essence in your everyday living. If you are stressed at work, you can take a moment to breathe out the tension, then step back into Essence and to see your coworkers or the conditions of your job from a different perspective. Chances are you will have a calmer response. As a parent, you might breathe out your tension and step back into Essence during moments of chaos to look upon your children with fresh eyes. Seeing the conditions of the situation clearly may inspire you to offer a wise, loving response in the chaos. You can also access Essence when you are dealing with difficult family members. How would Essence engage my angry brother or fussy aunt? When we are anchored in Essence, ease and clarity bring the Success Traits alive in our life.

When we are expressing our True Nature, peaceful, joyful, and content, we no longer spend our energy dodging our fears or proving our worth. When we are calm and centered, we don't have to attain a certain level of status, a great amount of money, praise, or accolades to feel "good enough." Satisfied and content, we measure our success through the joy and freedom we feel and the relationships and adventures we engage in that nourish our soul, bringing meaning and fulfillment to our lives. In other words, we fall in love with our own wondrous journey—just as Ryan was beginning to feel as he imagined stepping into the next chapter of his life supported by his Lifeforce.

When I first meet new clients, they typically tell me how miserable they are—the world is "too much" in some manner; it may be their job, their partner, or their family, or perhaps something is making them feel suffocated, unhappy, and miserable. *If I could just help them get rid of their problem, they'd be fine.* Instead, I offer an allegory: The world can be difficult, but our "problem" lies with the fact that we are cut off from our True Nature. It's as if each of us lives in a large, beautiful castle and the wings of the castle are our domains. As young children, we had the whole run of the castle. We played and explored all the rooms, even the rooms the grown-ups told us to stay away from! But as life went on, we encountered painful, scary experiences in different parts of the castle: We may have gotten our feelings hurt. We may have been injured while riding our bike. Maybe we were laughed at when we read our book report at school.

In an attempt to avoid our pain, many of us decided that it was best to never go into "that part" of the castle again. When our feelings got hurt, we may have decided to avoid people. Having crashed our bike, we may have avoided all physical activity in the hopes of never getting hurt again. After being shamed for our reading or writing, we may have given up on school. By the time my clients meet me, they've abandoned entire wings of their castle, effectively backing themselves into a broom closet. They may feel protected, but life feels miserable. Out of touch with the wisdom and expanse of their own beautiful Essence, life is both overwhelming and dull.

If we want to live a happy, successful life, we need to reclaim our castle. We need to go into the darkened wings and clear the cobwebs and pain so we can begin to live fully again. With Essence, we can light up those forgotten wings, for Essence possesses the strength, clarity, and wisdom to facilitate our healing and reawaken our aliveness, joy, and curiosity. When we begin to live fully in all our domains again, the wings of our castle light up, blazing with a wholistic intelligence—we are physically, psychologically, cognitively, socially, emotionally, and spiritually enlivened—which informs our choices and actions in ways that help us to realize our dreams and create successful outcomes.

The practices offered in True Success will help you clear the cobwebs and rediscover your own Essence so that you can realize your dreams and potential. How do we strengthen our connection to Essence? We do this through an investigation of the Seven Domains, for this is where our blocks reside—the ones that are keeping us from expressing our True Nature. As we locate these blocks and release them, we open the flow of Essence into all our domains, opening the door to truly successful living. Where to begin? Let's begin our journey with an exploration of the stories and beliefs that are shaping *and* limiting our lives, the Psychological Domain.

Section Two

True Success
in the
Seven Domains

The Psychological Domain
The Freedom to Live a New Story

If we want to create a truly successful life, we need a clear, sharp mind to advance our wishes, dreams, and values. When our mind is healthy and strong, we can confidently plan our future, learn new things, carry out strategies and projects, and handle the ups and downs that life brings. A happy, carefree mind emboldens us to try new adventures, step into new relationships, pursue our passions, and live our life as we are meant to live it—joyful, passionate, and inspired. In a truly successful life, a healthy mind serves as a keystone, anchoring our domains in strong, clear thinking.

The Psychological Domain is where we identify and work with the mind-states, beliefs, and opinions that drive our day-to-day choices and actions. *Psychology* is a Greek term originating from *psychē*, meaning "spirit/soul" and *logia*, pertaining to "reason" or "the study of," in other words, the study of our spirit. In today's world, psychology often

> The Psychological Domain is where we identify and work with the mind-states, beliefs, and opinions that drive our day-to-day choices and actions.

refers to the mental and behavioral characteristics of a person or group of people. What does psychology have to do with True Success? The thoughts and beliefs we form in our mind—about who we are and what life is about—greatly influence our choices, our dreams, and how we express ourselves in our domains. For example, if you believe that you are not deserving of love and friendship, it will be hard for you to thrive in the Relational Domain. If you believe that you have what it takes to qualify for a triathlon, you can persevere through the demanding workouts to excel in the Physical Domain. What we believe about ourselves and the world governs what we achieve in our domains and in life. For this reason, Mark and I see the Psychological Domain as a key element in creating True Success.

The inner stories and beliefs we carry in our mind have been crafted out of our life experiences. As we go through life, our mind classifies and makes meanings out of the events we encounter in order to make sense of our world. For instance, if you grew up with dogs and experienced a lot of joy and satisfaction playing with dogs, for you, "dog" means *fun*, *warmth*, *love*. But if you were attacked by a dog when you were young, there is a good chance "dog" means *teeth*, *biting*, *terror*. The personal meanings we make from our experiences go onto become beliefs and stories that dominate our mind, influencing our behavior and choices throughout our life. If you believe dogs are "awesome," you may own one. If dogs are "scary," you may go out of your way to avoid them at all costs. In this way, we are all being directed by the meanings that are entwined with our inner narratives.

We gather our inner scripts from a number of places. Some of our beliefs develop out of our personal aptitude and inclinations. If you could run fast as a child and won lots of races, you may believe, "Running is great!" But if you were a slow runner and were more inclined to sit in trees reading books, you may have decided, "Books are great!" Our inner narratives also arise out of our interactions with others. If you were told as a child, "You are a blessing!" your mind may be filled with thoughts that speak to your value, worth, and potential. But if you grew up hearing, "You're stupid...fat...lazy...worthless," these painful descriptions will mold your inner beliefs and attitudes.

Cultural and social norms also play a role in shaping our inner beliefs and stories. Our family's narratives about our culture, religion, race, or ethnic lineage may have created inner scripts that elicit feelings of pride, dignity, and a sense of belonging. Other stories may chronicle our family's pain: If our family has experienced racism, genocide, or fights for survival, we may carry stories that evoke feelings of fear or separation in relation to the broader culture. Societal norms also shape our beliefs and convictions. Being told what is "appropriate" or "expected" for women versus men...children and adults...married and single people...gay or straight people...human and the non-human world...those who possess wealth versus those who experience poverty... These societal directives color our perceptions of ourselves and others, governing what we believe is possible for people in their lifetime.

Our inner beliefs and stories are also shaped by our mental health and the traumas we've experienced. If we struggle with anxiety, depression, or mental illness, our inner stories will reflect the mental states that accompany these maladies: Anxiety brings worrisome thoughts; depression brings bleak or heavy thoughts; while other mental illnesses can bring chaos—our inner stories may be overshadowed by hatred, paranoia, mania, grief, and other strong emotions. Likewise, if we have experienced trauma, abuse, or injury, our terror and alarm can flood our mind with stories of fear, misfortune, and mistrust.

Embedded in these inner narratives are "instructions" that contain potent directives on how to live, what to believe, who we should be, and what we can and cannot do in our lifetime. Our inner scripts tell us what foods "delicious" and which ones are "disgusting." They tell us whom to socialize with, where to live, where to shop, what constitutes "good taste," whether to marry or whom, whom we should love or have sex with, and what work we should do in our lifetime. We may tell ourselves, "I have to get a college degree," or "I have to stay home and take care of my parents." We may chastise ourselves for our indulgences, "I can't spend that much money on myself!" or exclaim, "I can't live without that dress!" We may devoutly profess, "I'm Jewish, so I have to marry a Jewish person."

As such, our beliefs and inner directives shape the expression of who we think we are—they color our outlook, our personality, our mood, our behaviors, and how we view others. If we believe that we are *unwanted, unimportant,* and *unlovable,* we may label ourselves as a "loser" and find ourself shrinking away from people, spending lots of time alone, or engaging in mind-numbing habits such as drug abuse or overeating to quell our painful feelings. On the other hand, if we believe that we are *fun, inspiring,* and *have something to offer the world,* we may label ourselves as "popular" and happily go out and engage others, encouraging them to play with us. Our beliefs are also expressed in how we dress, the hairstyles we wear, the postures we adopt, and whom we socialize with. If your inner narrative declares that you are a Southern Baptist Christian, you will dress and act in a way that identifies you with your beliefs and congregation. If you see yourself as a Wall St. investment banker, you will conduct yourself in ways that align with that belief.

Since our beliefs are tied up in our sense of identity, it can feel like a matter of life-or-death when our narratives are challenged. Whether we know it or not, we are building our sense of purpose, justice, goodness, and spiritual worthiness on the meanings that fuel our beliefs, so any threat to our world view can elicit fierce protective instincts. A compelling example of this is found in the abortion debate. For some, abortion means *killing a baby* because the belief holds that a fully ensouled human exists from the moment of conception. For others, abortion means *the right of a woman to make decisions about her own body, her safety, and her personal choices in life.* These powerful meanings impel people to take fierce stands on either side of the debate, fueling religious clashes, divorces, political disputes, and family arguments across the dinner table. When it comes to our standing of goodness and our personal values, humans have been known to fight to the death over their meanings and beliefs.

While we are all governed by our inner narratives, the greater question is… Are these beliefs, *my* beliefs? Do they align with my true values and passions? If our beliefs reflect our deepest values, we are likely headed in the direction of a truly successful life. But if they are not our own—if our beliefs have been given to us by someone else, or they are driven by our fears instead of our truths—we may find ourselves living a life that is inauthentic or runs counter to our values and morals. To live a meaningful, authentic life, we need to clear our mind of any fearful or limiting beliefs that do not support our true standards and values. This is how we come to realize a truly successful life—we develop the skills that empower us to live in alignment with our values, morals, and aspirations.

Even when we attempt to live our authentic beliefs, it's not always easy to give up these inner directives. Our beliefs are strongly reinforced by our culture and society, and when we do try to step away from misaligned directives, we often feel a strong pull to uphold the values and edicts of our community. This is what happened to Walter. He wanted to join the Peace Corps, but in the end, he succumbed to his father's pressure, taking up the belief that "success" meant *money, power, and sexual promiscuity*—a notion that cost him his family and the fulfillment of a truly successful life.

To create a life that reflects our passions, values, and dreams, we need to cultivate a strong, healthy mind—a mind that can see clearly, examine its own beliefs, steady itself when times are tough, and savor the riches that we cultivate for ourselves. To cultivate a strong mind, we need to...

- Address the physical needs that support healthy brain functioning: In other words, we need to get enough sleep, eat well, and get enough exercise and movement.
- Understand the forces that shape our mind-states and beliefs.
- Recognize the beliefs and narratives that are holding us back in life and release them.
- Utilize supports such as psychotherapy and medication to stabilize our mind if we are struggling with anxiety, depression, or mental illness.
- Engage in healing practices to release any residual fear or pain if we have experienced trauma.

As we strengthen our mind and clear away the limiting beliefs and stories that are holding us back, we are free to create new narratives, ones built on our passions and the intelligence of our own True Nature. With authentic, inspiring narratives, we take the first steps to realizing the life that has been calling to us. The journey to creating a truly successful life is a journey into freedom—the freedom to be who we are meant to be.

Uncovering the Stories that Bind Us

Clarise was navigating her last semester of college when she came to see me for an appointment. "I don't know what's wrong with me," she said, flopping down on the couch. "Normally I'm fine in school, but I can't seem to focus, and I've got *a ton* of stuff to do before I graduate. I don't know what's going on."

"So, you did okay in school until this semester?" Clarise nodded. I noted to myself that she wasn't struggling with any inherent learning difficulties. "Has anything changed in the last months...any disruptive events or changes in your life, such as a relationship ending or being in an accident?"

Clarise shook her head. "No, everything's the same." She glanced around the room nervously, then grabbing a pillow off the couch, she hugged it close to her chest. "Every time I try to study, I just fog out and nothing gets done! I'm totally freaking out. I'm supposed to be graduating and..." She froze.

"And...what?"

Looking like a frightened little girl, she welled up with tears. "I don't know... What if I can't do it?! What if I can't handle being an adult?" She pulled the pillow closer and closed her eyes, as if blocking out her scary future.

I felt such tenderness for Clarise. She was standing at the edge of a new chapter in her life, but rather than feeling excited, she felt overwhelmed and unsure of herself. Something was making her fearful about stepping into this next phase. If she could release what was scaring her, I imagined she could open fully to her next adventure.

Offering a reassuring smile, I asked, "What comes up for you when you imagine life after graduation? What does 'life after graduation' *mean* to you?"

Clarise pulled her feet up onto the couch, encircling her legs and the pillow with her arms, making a tiny barrier between her and the world. "I don't know how to be an adult! I don't know what I'm supposed to do. I don't even know where I'm going to live after graduation! She burst into tears. "I just feel really scared!"

I handed her a tissue and placed the box next to her. "That's a lot of pressure, Clarise. Would it be okay if we took a moment to settle a little?" She nodded.

"So where are you noticing this fear and tension in your body right now?" She dabbed her eyes with the tissue. "There's a pounding in my chest."

I decided that a little mindfulness could help her settle. "Can you close your eyes and gently breathe out that tension that's pounding in your chest?" Nodding, she closed her eyes and began pushing her breath out in loud, determined puffs.

"I feel like the Little Engine Who Could," she said, smiling through her tears.

"You're doing just fine, but if you like, you can let your exhale be very gentle—more like, letting the fear and tension float off into space." I watched as Clarise's breath grew softer. "Now, as you do this, you might notice your body softening a bit." A moment later, she stretched her legs out, placing her feet on the floor.

"Take a moment to notice the feeling of your feet touching the floor; you can move them around a little if that helps you focus your attention there." Clarise flexed her feet a few times, then she rested her feet on the floor, releasing a long sigh.

"Just let your feet to sink into the floor, letting them rest in that support." I gave her a moment to savor the experience. "You may notice your feet feeling heavier, or they may be widening and softening as they relax."

I waited a few moments, then directed her attention to another source of support. "Notice where your back is touching the couch; you can let your weight sink into the cushions, resting in that support." Clarise sank deeply into the couch, resting her head on the cushions. Gently, I added, "You might also notice the support you're receiving from the pillow that you're holding against your chest." Clarise pulled the pillow up higher and rested her chin on it. She was now looking very comfortable and peaceful.

"So, as you settle here in this quiet, can you feel a sense of peace inside?" Clarise nodded. "If you like, you can begin breathing into this quiet peace, letting the peace get as big as it wants. You don't have to grow it, just allow it to expand on its own." I watched as her breath grew soft and steady. "If you like, you might imagine that you *are* this peace, so it's as if 'Peace' is breathing." She took a deep breath and exhaled slowly, growing very still.

"This peaceful spaciousness that you're experiencing is your own Essence. It's a quieter part of us that's always here in the background, just behind all the busyness. This part of us is always relaxed and at ease, even when life is stressful." I sat silently for a few moments, allowing Clarise to bask in the ease.

When we were finished with the exercise, Clarise opened her eyes. She looked relaxed and serene.

"I feel like I just took a warm bath. That was so relaxing."

"I'm glad you feel better. We just used a little mindfulness to shift your focus from your worries to the peace of your own inner Essence."

She wrinkled her nose. "Essence? I don't know about that word. For me, it felt more like a safe space or my *Being*."

I smiled. "Many people experience Essence as a safe space or a sense of Being. What's important to know is that when you are connected to your deeper inner Being, you'll be better equipped to deal with stress in your life. Are you familiar with mindfulness?"

Clarise shook her head. "I've read about it, but I've never done it."

"Mindfulness is a wonderful tool for cultivating inner strength and resilience. When we are being mindful, we focus our attention on our present moment experience—it helps us calm our mind so we can explore our experience at a deeper level to better understand what's happening in our life at any given moment. For example, when we were exploring the idea of you graduating, you started to worry about the future, which caused you to panic. I invited you to come back to the present moment—what is real, right now. In mindfulness practice, we focus on what *is*, not what *if*. In *this* moment, you have the support of peaceful breathing, the cushions on the couch, your feet resting on the floor...and

In mindfulness practice, we focus on what *is*, not what *if*.

relaxing in these supports allowed you to access the deeper peace of your inner Being. Anytime you release your tensions and center yourself in your Being, it will open a calm foundation that will help you negotiate new experiences successfully—even 'life after graduation.'"

Finding Peace with a Focused Mind

When you have some open time for yourself, find a comfortable position and close your eyes or look softly at the floor in front of you. Gently breathe out any stress or tension that you are noticing. When you feel ready, take a moment to feel the sensations in your feet—you can wiggle them if it helps you become more aware of how they feel. Are they warm or cold? Are they tight or relaxed? Take a moment to stretch and flex them, and then let them rest on the floor. How do they feel now? Allow yourself to receive the support of the floor, letting your feet get heavy and relaxed.

Next, place your awareness in the palms of your hands. You may notice some tingling, warmth, or pulsing. Whatever you notice, explore it with the curiosity of a young child. If you like, you can imagine the tingling or warmth rising out of your palms as you rest.

You can also place your awareness in your back, noticing the sensations in your back as you breathe in and out. You might notice a rising and falling sensation, or your back expands and contracts with each breath. Let yourself rest in that movement.

Finally, turn your attention to your mind. How does your mind feel after focusing on the sensations of your body? This practice often calms and settles the mind.

* * *

When we are mindful and in touch with our Essence, we possess a calm clarity that supports healthy mind-states. In True Success, Mark and I define mindfulness as *intentionally paying attention to present moment experience with clear awareness, a tender heart, and an open mind.* These qualities are in fact characteristics of Essence. Essence is inherently mindful, it sees things clearly, and holds a compassionate countenance. With its strong, calm foundation, we no longer have to rely on our beliefs for information, but we can see what is *actually* at play, so we can make clear, smart choices that lead to healthier, more successful outcomes.

For example, let's imagine that you carry an inner story that your boss is "scary." If you mindfully observe him as he is having a meltdown, you may notice that he doesn't look well. Seeing him clearly, you may feel compassion for him and step over your fear to offer him support—a much more mature, successful response. Mindfully watching your "tantruming" child, you may suddenly see their spirited, passionate heart, and filled with love, you may put aside your social beliefs about "disrespectful children" and sit on the floor to speak with them about their pain and their passions. If you believe that you have an "old, stiff body," mindfully stretching and moving your body may feel good, helping your body to become more pliant and flexible, creating a very different story from being "stiff and old." Whenever we become mindful and turn our attention away from our stories to what is true in a given moment, we see things with a fresh perspective, paving the way to a bigger, more enlivened life.

Uncovering the Roots of our Stories

When Clarise returned the following week, she looked discouraged. "I tried the mindfulness practice, but I couldn't feel Essence. I wasn't sure what I was looking for."

I smiled warmly. "That makes sense. You said that you didn't have a lot of experience with mindfulness, so it might take some time for you to do it on your own. The more you practice accessing Essence, or your *Being* in here, the easier it will be for you to access it at home. Basically, all we're doing is breathing out tension until you feel a little settled, and then notice any 'quiet' or 'comfort' within. When you find the 'quiet,' breathe into that comfort or peace, bringing it into focus. The more you play with letting 'Peace' breathe, the more you'll open to your sense of Being."

Clarise looked relieved. "I want to learn how to do it on my own because I'm still getting flustered. Last week I got a notice about caps and gowns and all my anxiety came back. I couldn't focus on my work, and I could barely think."

"Well, why don't we practice accessing Essence today. That way, you can get more familiar with opening to it yourself." Clarise nodded, so we spent the rest of that session practicing mindfulness, deepening to the inner peace that lay just beyond her anxious mind. By the end of the session, Clarise was feeling more confident about accessing her "Being."

When Clarise came back the following week, she was ready to work. "I touch into Essence!" She beamed for a moment, but quickly deflated. "But I'm still struggling with school—I still feel anxious every time I think about graduating."

"I'm not surprised you're still feeling anxious. We've worked on how to soothe your mind, but we haven't dealt with the fears concerning graduation. Let's use some mindfulness today and see if we can get to the root of what's troubling you. Once we address these fears or stressors, I think you'll get back on track with your studies." I threw her a playful smile. "You might even look forward to graduating!"

Clarise wrinkled her nose. "You think so?! I don't know about that…"

I laughed. "You might find that releasing your fears gives you a new lease on life!"

I invited Clarise to get comfortable and close her eyes. Before settling in, she reached for "her" pillow and hugged it; when she was comfy, she closed her eyes.

"So, take a few breaths and release any tension that you're holding in your body, mind or heart." I paused, giving her a moment to settle. When she looked restful and mindful, I continued. "Now I'm going to say some words, and as I say them, you just notice what comes up in your mind and body when you hear them."

"So, notice what happens when you hear, 'Graduation is almost here.'" Clarise stiffened and held her breath.

"Can you sense that tightening?"

She nodded. "Yeah, I feel scared."

"And where do you feel that fear in your body? Is it in your stomach, your head, your heart?"

"I feel it in my chest. It feels like a burning ball of fire."

"Okay... Now imagine for a moment that you're that ball of fire." I paused to let her feel the sensations. "I say, 'Graduation is almost here,' and if this ball of fire could talk, what would it say?"

She frowned. "It's yelling, 'I can't do this! I can't do this!'"

"And how old does this voice feel, the one who's yelling, 'I can't do this?'"

"Little... like five."

"And is this five-year-old standing in a particular place?"

She paused a moment, then said, "I'm in the school yard. It's the first day of kindergarten." Tearing up, she spoke in a voice that sounded like a little girl. "My mom left, and I don't know these people! I don't know what's happening!"

Gently engaging the little girl, I said, "The first day of kindergarten can be very scary. I'm sorry your mom left you in the schoolyard."

Clarise nodded. "The teacher is telling us to line up and I don't know what to do!"

Clarise's kindergarten story was still alive inside her, scripting her life as a young adult. For Clarise, "graduating college" was bringing up feelings from another time when she stood on the edge of another unknown future, her first day of kindergarten. The anxiety, loss, and confusion she felt as a five-year-old was framing her response to her current situation. No wonder she couldn't study.

* * *

As we go through life, our brain is continually accessing memories to gather information on how we should respond in the present moment.

We see a car drive past us, and our mind quickly scans our memories for everything we know about cars—makes and models, how to drive, or perhaps an interesting fact about that particular car. If we note nothing of immediate relevance to us, we turn our attention elsewhere. But if the car driving by looks just like our ex-partner's car, the information about "car" is suddenly entangled with memories and feelings about our ex-partner. We may suddenly feel anxious and unsettled, and in our mind, we may jump right back into the relationship, arguing with our ex in our head. For Clarise, the prospect of leaving her "known" familiar life—the comfort and safety of campus, classes, and school friends—was bringing up old anxiety that she experienced long ago when she had to leave the comfort and familiarity of her home to enter the world of kindergarten. As she was getting ready to leave college, not only was she feeling her fear of the present unknown, she was also feeling the overwhelm of a five-year-old.

Embedded in our memories is a whole collection of "earlier me's" that can spring to life under the right circumstances. If someone brings out a spectacular birthday cake, we may squeal with delight like an excited child, feeling just as we did on birthdays long ago. If our boss yells during a meeting, we may instantly flash to our father's harsh voice, feeling like a kid in trouble. Our partner may touch us in a certain way, and we cringe, suddenly transported to the backseat of an old boyfriend's car, pushing off the advances of a groping adolescent boy. Or we may feel a stabbing pain in our stomach and clench in terror, convinced that the cancer we had twelve years ago, is back. Our experiences and responses in the present are often replays of our earlier life; when the conditions are "just right," earlier memories open, driving our responses in the present.

In the world of psychology, this earlier me is known by many names—*our inner child, small self, sub-personalities,* or *personas.* However, I find a term from Buddhist psychology most useful: "mental formations." In Buddhist psychology, mental formations refer to anything we experience with our mind—thoughts, ideas, sensations, feelings, and the perceptions we experience through seeing, hearing, tasting, etc. From this perspective, any memory or belief from the past that personifies as "me" in the present moment (meaning that we temporarily experience that I *am* four years old, fifteen years old, or "me" from last week) is a mental formation.

We can think of formations as wounded, frozen, unresolved, unintegrated memories that are stored in our mind and body. They arise as flashes of memory, impulses, beliefs, and behavioral and relational patterns that color our experience and our actions in ways that usually don't serve us, or others. We can think of them as representations of a *fictional self,* what I like to call, "Me Inc." —the habits and personality we have that is reactive to the world—not our True Nature. Our True Nature is present-focused, anchored in the calm of Essence, and it responds to the world with wisdom and clear thinking. Formations operate more like frightened or irritated children.

Formations arise anytime the conditions in the present are *similar enough* to a past event. If we feel overwhelmed writing a report for work, we may suddenly feel like a defeated school kid doing homework: "I can't do this!" When a driver cuts us off in traffic, we may instantly become an enraged teenager: "Yeah?! Well, Fuck You!!" If we don't get our way with our partner, we may pout like a five-year-old or yell and stomp our feet. And if life feels overwhelming, we may collapse in tears, like a small child. When we are caught up in our formations, we don't see the world as it is, but rather as "earlier me" saw it years ago.

Anytime we react with a less than ideal response, there is a formation involved. If we overreact when someone corrects us...freeze and don't help in a moment of trauma...overeat when our feelings are hurt...drink alcohol to excess when we're out socializing...use drugs to numb out when we're mad...or scream or hit someone when we don't get our way, we are caught in a flare up of "earlier me," entranced by a past memory. It is only later, when the trance has released, that we lament, "I can't believe I just did that!" We have just acted out our past, in present time.

Mental formations can arise in many guises. The most familiar form is that of a young inner child. However, formations come in other shapes as well. Making a mistake, we may hear a critical voice in our head—the sharp, angry voice of a parent or critical authority figure. They can come as memories—watching a scary movie, we may suddenly flash to a frightening scene from our own past. They may come as sensations—feeling nervous about a new venture, we may feel nauseous or feel "butterflies" in our stomach. And formations can also appear as intense emotions such as anxiety, shame, or depression, and sometimes, they may even take the form of objects. Like Clarise, we may feel a "ball of fire" in our chest, or a "rock" in our stomach, a "tornado" inside us, or a "tiger" crouching, ready to attack.

If we want to create a truly successful life, it is vital that we release the old narratives and beliefs that have us locked in outdated scripts. When we realize that our reactions are replays of old memories that are no longer true in our present life, we can free ourselves to make room for new information and beliefs that support successful living. Without our old fearful storylines, we can embody the strength, joy, and intelligence of a healthy adult, and authentically express our values, our passions, and our true potential.

New Identity / New Story

When Clarise discovered the formation of the little girl standing all alone on that first day of kindergarten, she had uncovered the root of her problem. She was seeing her current life transition—graduating from college—through the eyes of a little girl who didn't have the knowledge or capacity to negotiate an adult life; that is why she was wailing, "I don't know what to do!" As a graduating senior, Clarise was at a phase of her life when adulthood should be embraced as an exciting adventure. To navigate her new future as a healthy young adult, she needed to release the little girl formation and discover the part of her that would welcome stepping into the "Great Unknown."

To help Clarise untangle herself from her five-year-old overwhelm, I invited her to settle. "Can you feel the fear and sadness inside you?" She nodded, looking very much like a little girl. "Why don't you take a moment to breathe out that fear and sadness. You don't have to hold onto it." She exhaled a couple of shaky breaths, then her breathing softened. When she seemed more relaxed, I invited her to touch into Essence.

"So as you're breathing out that tension, can you notice some quiet inside?" She nodded. "Let yourself 'step back' into that quiet and begin breathing there..." A few moments later, she looked very still. "What are you noticing now?"

Almost in a whisper, she said, "I can feel my Being. It's very calm."

By shifting her identity from the scared little girl to her Being, Clarise had taken the first step in writing a new story. "As you're resting in your Being, I'd like you to let it access this memory in the schoolyard. Your mom has left...and you're standing in your Being, looking around the schoolyard, watching the other kids lining up." Clarise sighed softly and she leaned back into the couch.

"As you're taking in this scene, grounded in Being, I'd like you to notice... Is your Being five years old?"

Clarise shook her head. "No. It doesn't have an age."

"Is your Being overwhelmed, or feeling like, 'I can't handle this'?"

With her eyes still closed, she smiled, "No, it's calm."

"So this deeper part of you is not five years old, it's not overwhelmed; it's calm and centered. The deepest part of you is absolutely fine." I let that sink in.

"This five-year-old has been frozen in this schoolyard for decades, scared and sad. And yet your Being can handle this situation. Would the five-year-old like to let your Being take over so she can leave this place that feels scary? She doesn't have to stay in this memory forever."

Clarise didn't hesitate. "She wants to leave. She hates this place."

"Okay, so let's imagine that she can leave and no longer has to be a scared, little girl. If she could become anything that would make her feel safe and happy—she could be a butterfly...the wind flying free...a puppy, snuggling on someone's lap...or she could go play with someone she really likes... What would feel good to her?"

Clarise reflected a moment, then she brightly said, "She wants to be a butterfly!"

"That sounds perfect—so free and easy going! So, to become a butterfly, all she has to do is let go of this form of the frightened little girl. Would she be willing to let go of this form so that she could be a butterfly? Forms can always change; they're just energy structures. As Einstein pointed out, energy never dies, it just changes form."

Clarise nodded decisively. "She wants to be a butterfly!"

"Then take a moment to feel the little girl inside you; she's standing in the school yard... And as you feel her body, imagine it becomes tingling energy. She might even enjoy just being tingly energy for a moment." I gave her a moment to savor the experience. "When you feel ready, allow the energy to 'bubble' out of your body. As the energy leaves, you might feel some tingling, or heat rising off your body, or you may feel pressure releasing from your body." I gave her a moment to feel the release of the formation. "If you like, you can imagine the energy changing into a carefree butterfly." I watched as Clarise softened with each exhale. "Can you feel the energy leaving your body?" She nodded. "Where is the energy leaving from?"

Quietly, she murmured, "I feel a tingling going out of my chest."

"Wonderful. And as this energy is leaving your body, I'd like you to notice something. Do you feel as if you're shrinking or fading?"

Clarise shook her head. "No, I feel bigger."

"This is important to see, as the little girl is a *memory*. If she were "you," you'd be shrinking and fading as she leaves. You are not losing a part of yourself; you're just releasing the old fear and pain associated with an anxious memory. So you can relax and just let all the energy release." With my invitation, Clarise sank into the couch, spreading her arms across the cushions, expanding her chest.

"You might also imagine the butterfly flitting from flower to flower on a warm summer day." With her eyes closed, Clarise smiled.

With the formation released, I invited Clarise to one last exploration. "Now that the five-year-old has left, I'd like you to notice two qualities that are present right now for you."

With a confident voice, she said, "I feel calm and strong."

"That sounds wonderful. Take a moment to breathe this feeling of strength and calm throughout your body so you can anchor it within you. In this moment, your Being is expressing itself as calm strength."

Now that Clarise was anchored in Essence, she was ready to address her current issue. "So as you embody this calm strength, resting in your Being, notice what happens when I say, 'Graduation is coming.' Is your inner Being worried about this?"

Clarise shook her head. "No, it's peaceful. Actually, it feels a little excited." She smiled, then opened her eyes. "This is cool!"

I smiled back. "It is cool! When we let go of our old fears and rest in our deeper Being, life gets a lot easier."

As I explained to Clarise, the fearful formations of her past—the ones that make up "Clarise Inc.," are not her True Nature. "Clarise Inc." is a fictionalized representation. As long as she believed that deep down, she was a scared little girl, she wouldn't be able to live her life fully. Releasing her fearful formation and landing in her Essence awakened the Success Traits; she was now feeling calm and strong, attributes that would help her succeed as an adult. With "calm strength" Clarise could step into her unknown future and pursue all her dreams and aspirations.

As we wrapped up our session that day, I offered a suggestion: "During this next week, see if you can touch into this calm strength as you do your schoolwork. If anything stressful comes up about graduation, try breathing out the tension, and step back into your Being."

She smiled brightly. "Okay! I'm excited to see how it works!"

Clarise came back to see me a few more times, and we worked to release other formations that were frightening and overwhelming to her. Over time, she began to settle more deeply into her Essence, taking on a more confident presence. One day, as we were finishing up a session, I asked how her studies were going.

"It's going really well! I'm back on top of my classes and my focus is a lot better. Whenever I get overwhelmed, I breathe out my stress, and if that doesn't work, I find the formation that's freaking out inside. Instead of getting all tangled up in the fear, I just step into Being and asked, 'Is my Being freaking out about this?' Nope! My Being is fine! So, I release the one who's scared—letting them turn into butterflies, puppies, whatever—and I get back to work. I'm actually excited about graduating! I'm starting to think about what I want to do with my life."

I gave her a warm, encouraging smile. "It can be exciting to think about your future...and it's okay if you don't figure it all out right away. Often, I find that life unfolds in its own time. We don't really *dictate* our life, we *discover* our life, and it can be an exciting journey! As long as you keep clearing your formations and resting in your Being, you'll have the clarity, wisdom and strength you need to meet life and follow your dreams as they unfold."

As Clarise shows us, we don't need to get "all tangled up" in our fears and doubts. We can release our limiting stories and create our own True Success. With these kinds of practices, we can write a new story, one that allows us to build a life that is fun and meaningful for us.

Is there some area of your life that you would like to expand into, but you find yourself hesitant or a little afraid? Perhaps you want to ask for a promotion, or you dream of moving to a new place. Maybe you would like to retire, or you want to jump into a new venture. You can begin your journey by taking up the soothing practices offered in this chapter, perhaps beginning with a mindfulness practice. Take some time each day to close your eyes and gently breathe out your tension or stress, and when you feel ready, rest in the supports around you: Let your feet sink into the floor, or give your full weight to the chair you are sitting in. If you are outdoors, rest in the sound of birds singing or savor the feeling of the breeze on your face. You can also rest in the gentle rise and fall of your breath. Resting in these supports will allow your mind to settle.

Once you feel comfortable with mindfulness practice, you can develop your connection to Essence. After breathing out your tension, notice where you sense some peace or quiet within. Gently breathe into that space, allowing the peace or quiet to get as big as it wants. You can then let yourself *become* the peaceful Quiet, imagining that "Peace" is breathing. This is the embodiment that opens us to Essence. Once you are anchored in Essence, rest as long as you like, savoring the deep inner peace. Doing these practices will give you a great foundation for release work.

When you feel ready to practice releasing formations, you can follow the steps laid out in the acronym S.U.C.C.ESS.

Soothe—When you find yourself stuck in a limiting story or belief, take a moment to breathe out the tension you are noticing and relax in the supports around you—the comfort of your chair, resting in the rise and fall of your breath, or resting your hands on your lap. Ground yourself in the peace and ease of these supports.

Uncover the Formation—Return to the hindering belief/story and notice any sensations or feelings that are present. Is there a rumbling in your stomach...a restless energy...is your jaw clenched? If these sensations could talk, what would they say? Is the voice that is speaking a certain age? Is this younger one standing in a particular place? These questions may open a memory.

Check in with Essence—Take a couple of calming breaths and "step back" into the peace and ease of Essence. When you are anchored in Essence, ask yourself, "Is Essence upset or overwhelmed by this experience? Is Essence the age of this formation?" Note that the deepest part of you, your Essence, is okay.

Clear the Formation—Grounded in the clarity of Essence, the formation no longer has to remain in this difficult memory—Essence can handle our stressful moments. What would feel nourishing and healing for this "earlier me?" When an answer arises, allow the formation to become "energy," and release out of your body so it can take on this nourishing experience. As the formation releases, you may feel some tingling or energy "bubbling out," heat rising off your body, or pressure releasing as the energy leaves.

ESSence remains. Let yourself rest in the peace and ease of Essence. What qualities are present now? Take some time to breathe these stabilizing qualities throughout your body in order to anchor them. Grounded in these qualities, now turn your attention to your initial stressor. How does Essence relate to this stressor; how does it envision dealing with this situation? What actions might you take that are aligned with your True Nature?

An important note about releasing formations: If you want to practice releasing formations, it's important to begin with small irritations and frustrations initially. It is not advisable to begin this work with fearful or traumatic memories. Instead, pick something that irritates you, like spilling your coffee. When you spill your coffee, do you sigh and get something to wipe it up, or do you curse and stomp your feet? If the latter, there's a formation activated that you might want to release. Let yourself find the "earlier me" who curses when things go awry and work through the S.U.C.C.ESS steps. It is also important that you not begin with strong sensations or chronic pain in your body for stronger sensations tend to relate to bigger, more painful stories and memories. As your foundation in these practices grows and your connection to Essence strengthens, you will be able to release bigger stories, but for now, practice with irritations. If you are often overwhelmed with big feelings, such as fear, anxiety, or depression, you can focus on breathing out your tension to settle yourself. If you struggle with trauma or overwhelming experiences, you may want to seek out the support of a psychotherapist or healer. Getting support is an important part of a truly successful life.

Once you are comfortable releasing formations, you can release them at any moment in your life—while sitting in a meeting, at the dinner table with your family, or sitting in traffic. You can also release formations while running, working quietly in your garden, doing yoga, getting a massage, dancing, or meditating. For instance, I often do releases while I'm swimming. As I quietly swim laps, I notice any stress or formations that are plaguing me that day and ask the formations what new form would feel healing and nourishing. I then allow the energy to gently release as I swim. Doing this allows me to feel more relaxed, and as I settle into Essence, solutions to my stressful situations often appear as I'm swimming.

One of the most effective ways to release formations is to practice while lying down in meditation. When we are lying down, we don't need to hold ourselves up in any way which allows for a more complete release of tension. If you choose to do a lying down meditation, make sure to place a pillow or bolster under your knees, as this will allow your lower back to drop, making you more comfortable.

With the release of our limiting formations, we liberate ourselves from "Me Inc.'s" story and open ourselves to writing a new story: *Connected with Essence, I can release my fears and outdated beliefs to meet life with clarity, strength, and compassion, creating the life I'm meant to live.* With this story, we can develop any domain—we can develop our physical capabilities, our cognitive aptitude, our emotional fluidity, our relational freedom, and our spiritual capacity, empowering us to realize a vibrant, meaningful, authentic life.

As you step into the Psychological Domain and cultivate a clear, strong mind, your True Nature will begin to shine more readily. With a clear, relaxed, healthy mind, you can begin making choices that will open doors to your passions and ambitions: You may choose to go back to school or move to a different place. You may begin a new relationship, go on an adventure, or apply for a new job. You might commit yourself to a cause that is dear to your heart. Like Clarise, you can jump into new territory, assured that you can handle what's coming as you cultivate the wisdom and skills you'll need to realize your heart's desires. With a clear, bright mind, you have the inner light to illuminate every room of your castle, delighting in your domains, joyful, confident, and excited to be alive. This is the Essence of True Success—the freedom to write yourself a new story.

The Physical Domain
The Freedom to Be Fully Alive

One of the most precious gifts in life is having a body. Through our body we enjoy our favorite foods, snuggle with loved ones, delight in the feeling of rain splashing on our face, and relish the scent of crisp autumn leaves. Our body also expresses our passions, our joys, and our sorrows—we squeal with delight, cry with pain, wail with heartache, show our kindness in a smile, and our displeasure in a frown. In our eyes, voice, and gestures, we reveal our unique spirit, just as our distinct fingerprints and DNA reveal our genetics. We also express our beliefs and emotions in how we dress our body—we may wear our favorite team hat, our "Save the Planet" tee-shirt, or a floral dress that proclaims to the world, "I LOVE flowers!" Through the gift of our body, we get to meet and experience the world as human beings.

On the road to True Success, the Physical Domain is where we cultivate our body and physical expression to its fullest potential. Here, we address our physical aptitude, movement, exercise, our health, and the care and enjoyment of our body. We also work with the psychological beliefs that have shaped our physical life—for better or worse—as our attitudes and conditioning greatly influence our health, vibrancy, and functioning. Our relationship with our body determines the vitality of our aliveness and our physical competence as we endeavor to express a healthy, successful life.

As you reflect on your physical expression, in what areas do you shine? Perhaps you love dancing, building things, or making art. You may be passionate about sex, or you cherish sensual experiences—you love breathing in the scent of flowers, swimming in a cool lake, soaking up warm sunshine, or basking in the sights and sounds of a city neighborhood. Perhaps you are an athlete who enjoys the rush of adrenaline and the feeling of strength as you push your body to the limit. Or you may have a strong body that can work for hours. When we are delighting in physical activity, we discover a joy and playfulness that unveils our True Nature and life feels vibrant and sparkly.

In what ways might you struggle in this domain? Perhaps you do not like your body, or you wish that your body looked different. You may have been shamed about the size of your body, its shape, the way it moves, or the color of your skin. You may wish that your body performed differently; you find it difficult to move or do simple tasks. This often happens when we suffer from physical disabilities, chronic illness, pain, or when we are out of shape or struggle with our weight. Perhaps you suffer from addictions that are ruining your health and well-being. Or maybe you don't like the way your body is aging. Perhaps you've endured physical or sexual abuse, complicating your relationship with your body; you want to feel safe in your body, but your body is a source of pain and sadness.

If you struggle in this domain, you may try to avoid the whole physical wing of your castle, choosing instead to live out your life in other domains. For instance, you might live "up in your head," far away from your body, focusing exclusively on the musings of your Cognitive Domain; you may fill your days with thinking, reading, working on computers, or philosophizing about the world—far more comfortable with your thoughts than your physical experience. Or you may spend your days in the Social-Relational Domain—socializing with friends, talking on the phone, doing Zoom meetings—never engaging in a conscious relationship with your body. Disconnected from your body, you may have developed some unhealthy habits: Perhaps you are not eating well or exercising, not taking time to rest, or at the end of the day, your self-care is ruled by weariness—you find yourself flipping through your phone screen, playing video games, watching TV while eating, or falling asleep on the couch.

If this describes your physical life, you are not alone. In the last twenty years, many of us have become disconnected from our body. A recent survey by the US Department of Labor found that roughly 80 percent of US citizens do not regularly participate in sports, exercise, or physical recreation. Another survey reported that most people in the United States spend over 50 percent of their leisure time watching television. (This doesn't include time spent on the Internet.) When our life is consumed by so much screen time, it's hard to manifest a vital, healthy body. The Mayo Clinic recently reported that those who sit eight hours or more a day have the same health risks as those who struggle with obesity and smoking. And to complicate matters, obesity is on the rise: Obesity rates across the world have been steadily climbing over the last twenty years. Sadly, fewer and fewer of us are going outdoors and enjoying a physical life.

Beyond our sedentary lifestyle, other influences are negatively impacting our physical health. Increases in advertisements for quick-and-easy snack foods have resulted in more people turning to processed meals (higher in sugar, calories, and chemicals), while eating fewer fresh foods and vegetables. And for some, fresh fruits and vegetables are even hard to come by in their communities. Recent studies have revealed that supermarkets in economically depressed neighborhoods tend to carry less healthy foods. Add to this food insecurity (not having enough to eat) and the high cost of organically grown foods, and many people find healthy eating out of reach.

Our physical health is also compromised by other factors. Today, many people find themselves overwhelmed by the demands of modern life, making it difficult to attend to their own self-care. Every overextended parent or caretaker knows how hard it is to carve out some "me time" to rest, eat well, and get some exercise. Additionally, many people are struggling with mental stressors that trigger unhealthy behaviors such as overeating, substance abuse, self-harming, anorexia, or bulimia. And our social media is also contributing to our ill-health: As more people compare themselves against photoshopped images, we have seen increases in depression and body dysmorphia (obsessing about perceived defects in our appearance), which have led to increases in starvation diets and plastic surgery. And every day in communities across the world, physical health is threatened by poverty, pollution, toxins, and limited access to healthcare. Given these hinderances to our physical health, it is clear that we need to take an active role in securing our physical well-being—it is up to us to reclaim our physical health.

We often hear, "Having your health is the most important thing." In moments when we are suffering from pain or illness, we know the truth of these words. When we are physically suffering, life can feel miserable and it can be hard to function—our physical health can impact our cognitive thinking, our emotional stability, our psychological processing, our ability to socialize, and our capacity for spiritual practice. A healthy, active body supports our functioning in life and in all our domains. This doesn't mean that True Success is available only to athletes, yoga teachers, those in top physical shape and great health. On the contrary, we can manifest a truly successful life even when we struggle with physical issues. But since our domains are interconnected, our physical health and vitality does give our domains the best chance for thriving and developing, making our life easier and more enjoyable.

Taking Time to Meet Your Body

When you have some time, take a moment to breathe out your tension and relax. When you feel ready, write down five beliefs or attitudes that define your body or your physical life. For example: *I love my body...I love sports...I love sex!* Or *I hate my body...I have to have a perfect body...I'm fat...I'm ugly...I hate exercise! I look silly dancing... singing...having sex...*These are some of the beliefs that are driving your physical domain.

As you reflect on these narratives, do they bring your closer to your body or do they make you want to draw away from your body? Where did you get these beliefs? Do you recall any memories that might be related to these narratives? Note how your physical past is coloring your present physical life. If you are holding any painful narratives, know that it's possible to release the formations that are fueling these beliefs to rewrite a new physical story. How does it make you feel, knowing that you can rewrite your physical story?

As you reflect on your Physical Domain, what would help you live a more vibrant, healthy life? Perhaps you want to get in shape, get outdoors more, or increase your mobility. You may want to pick up a sport or cultivate an exercise routine. Maybe you would like to take better care of your body, or you want to fall in love with your body, giving it all the love, care, respect, and tenderness it deserves. Perhaps more aliveness would come from expressing yourself freely in your body: You would love to dance with abandonment, dress more playfully, enjoy sex, or just have more physical freedom. If you are an athlete, you may dream of improving your performance or bringing your game up to the next level. When we develop a healthy, conscious relationship with our body, it becomes a wonderful vehicle for living more fully and enjoying True Success.

Learning to Listen to Our Body

On a bright spring morning, Jen pranced into my office wearing a feathered boa and a sparkly leotard encircled by a purple tutu. She was a large, strong woman, yet she breezed past me with a lightness and joy that invited a certain playfulness. "Nice tutu," I commented. She turned, smiling brightly. "Thank you! I just came from a science fair. Kids learn better when you mix science with entertainment!"

I smiled, amused. "I'm sure they appreciated your efforts!"

Jen beamed. "They did! I had the most popular exhibit, and they learned a lot!"

Sitting on the couch, Jen was careful not to crush her tutu, and she occasionally fluffed it as she shared her story with me. Immediately, she jumped into telling me about her parents—they were lifelong addicts and her mother had been particularly mean, having picked on Jen her entire life. "They're both a mess, but my mom's the worst; she's always on me. Nothing's ever good enough for her."

Jen left home when she was sixteen, working hard to support herself. In time, she earned a master's degree, landing a job as a middle school science teacher. She loved teaching and had worked hard to create a stable life; she rarely saw her parents, as they lived on the other side of the country, and to this day, she had little contact with them.

"And that's exactly how I like it," she said.

As we continued talking, it became clear that there was more to her story than the difficulties with her parents.

"So, why exactly did you want to see me?"

Jen brushed some sparkles off her tutu. "Oh, I don't know. I guess I'm not happy with my life."

I nodded supportively. "And why aren't you happy with your life?" Jen's eyes widened, "Are you kidding me? You're a therapist, right?! Look at me—I'm fat and I'm dressed in a purple tutu. Does that give you a clue?" She playfully raised her eyebrows, as if she was reconsidering my credentials. "Look, I'm an advocate for body positivity—that's why I wear leotards, tutus and boas. And parts of my life are going really well;

I love teaching and I love my students. But outside of teaching, my life is a mess. I'm not a healthy weight, my blood pressure's not good, and at the end of my school day, I do *nothing*. I grade papers...make up lesson plans...and eat." She looked down and nervously fluffed her tutu. "Oh, who am I kidding? I eat all day. I'm so busy at work, I just grab snacks on the run—potato chips, stuff out of the vending machine, anything to keep going. That teachers' lounge is a 'fathole;' you know, like a blackhole but... You get it. I swear there's a gravitational pull when I walk by that lounge, and then there's that little voice in my head... *Let's just pop in and see what they have today. Oooh, Look! Pecan Rolls!*" She rolled her eyes sarcastically. Then in all seriousness, she said, "Some parts of my life are so awesome, but other parts are just a mess."

I felt such compassion for Jen. Here was a bright, funny, creative woman—so alive and talented—and yet, she wasn't happy, and she wasn't living what she would consider to be a truly successful life. She clearly shined as a teacher, but her self-effacing beliefs and her difficulties with eating were keeping her from landing fully in her True Nature. If she could resolve the issues behind her physical struggles, I knew she could bring her vitality and joy into other areas of her life to enliven her personal life.

"Jen, so many parts of your life are working well and it's clear that you have many gifts." She shook her head resolutely, "No, *some* things are working well—I know I'm a good teacher. But if you saw me at night with a tub of Bing Cherry Madness, you'd think otherwise."

I smiled kindly, questioning her conclusion. "I don't know about that... I see a woman who is smart, funny, gifted and rather hard on herself. I imagine there's a good reason for your difficulties, but that's why you're here—so we can discover the root of those issues and resolve them." I spent some time gathering additional information about her life and then introduced Jen to the Seven Domains so she could better understand why she was doing so well in some areas, while struggling in others.

When Jen was finished mapping out her domains, she looked up smiling. As I suspected, Jen was strongly developed in the Cognitive,

Psychological, and Spiritual Domains. Not surprisingly, she was struggling in the Physical and Emotional domains. Interestingly, in the Social-Relational domain her profile was "mixed:" She was socially gifted as a teacher, but in her personal life, she didn't have any intimate relationships. I imagined this was related to her parents' substance abuse and her mother's aversive behavior.

Jen was happy seeing her strengths, but she quickly collapsed. "Looking at these domains, it's clear that I use all my strengths at work; but personally, it shows that I'm a mess."

I smiled kindly. "I think you're just like everyone else. In the domains where we excel, we've had lots of support or we possess natural talent; in the domains where we struggle, we've usually experienced a lot of pain or a lack of support."

"Let me ask you something... If you're working with a kid who is struggling in science and they tell you that they're a 'mess,' do you believe them?"

Jen smiled, savvy to where this was going. "Obviously not! A mind can never learn while it's busy beating itself up. I would help that student relax and then I'd offer them a different avenue for learning."

I grinned. "Exactly! And that's what we do here! Let me show you a practice that can help you relax. It might soften some of the judgments you're having about yourself and help you..."

"Stop eating Bing Cherry Madness?"

I smiled. "Maybe...but I was thinking more along the lines of bringing in some self-compassion. The practice is known as *Loving Kindness*. It's a mindfulness practice that's been around for centuries to help soothe the mind and body when there's stress. Would you like to try it?"

Jen nodded earnestly. "Sure, if it helps me get my life on track."

I invited Jen to get comfortable and close her eyes. "So, I'm going to say some phrases, and after each phrase, I'll pause so you can repeat the words quietly to yourself. We'll run through the practice three times, so you can let the words sink in deeply." She nestled into the couch, getting comfy. When she was settled, I recited the phrases.

"May I be filled with loving-kindness."

"May I be peaceful and at ease."

"May I be well and healthy."

"May I be safe from inner harm and outer harm."

"May I be free."

"May I be happy and content."

And to help Jen connect with her body, I added another phrase in support of her healing: "May I care for myself with kindness and with love." When we finished, Jen was resting peacefully with her eyes closed.

"So, how are you feeling?"

She smiled softly. "Really calm and peaceful."

"If you like, you can breathe this peaceful calm throughout your body—into your feet and legs...your torso...your cells...allowing your whole being to fill with this peace."

She took a couple of deep breaths, exhaling slowly. When she opened her eyes, her face was soft, and she was deeply nestled in the cushions. "I've never felt like this. I feel really safe and happy, like everything's going to be okay."

"Loving Kindness is a great practice. It helps us shift our focus from stressful thoughts to kind sentiments that invite natural healing, bringing ease and nourishment to our system. If you take some time each day to recite these phrases, you'll soon notice a peace and calm that stays with you longer and longer throughout your day. Once you memorize the phrases, you can take them into your life: You can say them when you're stressed at work, when you're stuck in traffic, even when you're eating a tub of Bing Cherry Madness."

Jen smiled gratefully. "That would be nice. Usually, I just beat myself up when I cave into cravings."

For the rest of that session, we focused on Essence so Jen would have a strong, reliable foundation when we deepened into the blocks and fears that lay behind her struggles. As we wrapped up our session, I handed her a copy of the Loving Kindness phrases. "If you practice with Loving Kindness and Essence, you'll have a great foundation for our work going forward."

Jen smiled, holding up the card. "This is going with me, everywhere!"

As you engage in your own personal healing, you may want to offer Loving Kindness to yourself. In a quiet moment, read through the phrases, feeling into the intention of the words. You can also "breathe in" each phrase, letting it anchor deep inside you. I find that doing the practice three times greatly deepens the peace and ease, but do it as long as you like. When you finish reciting the phrases, take a moment to breathe the peace and ease throughout your body, anchoring it within you. Once you memorize the phrases, you can take them into your daily life. Notice how Loving Kindness affects your mood, your physical well-being, and your experience of stress. Doing this practice will gently rewire your mind and body for greater health and well-being.

Loving Kindness

When you have a moment, take some time to recite these phrases.
Doing this practice three times can deepen the positive feelings.

May I be filled with loving-kindness.
May I be peaceful and at ease.
May I be well and healthy.
May I be safe from inner harm and outer harm.
May I be free.
May I be happy and content.
Notice how you feel having bathed yourself in these kind intentions.

Meeting Our Body with Kindness

After a couple of weeks of working with Essence and Loving Kindness, Jen was eager to work. I invited her to close her eyes and guided her in a brief mindfulness practice to help her settle, then asked her to shift her attention to her body.

"So as you focus on your body, what comes into your awareness most strongly?"

Jen frowned. "Fat. And it's disgusting."

"Would it be okay to work with this 'fat' that you're noticing? You said that you'd like to have a healthier weight."

Jen scowled, "Yeah, I'm sick of it."

Gently, I said, "As we go forward in this work Jen, I'd like to invite you to hold a soft, gentle attitude in our explorations, for we often find something tender as we deepen down."

With her eyes still closed, Jen cringed. "But I don't like fat."

"I can see how that might be true. But let's imagine for a moment that this fat has a purpose; that it's here for a reason."

She shook her head doggedly. "It's just a big wall of fat. I don't see what its purpose is."

"Well, let's deepen down and explore that. Imagine for a moment that you can 'be' this wall of fat. Don't *think*. Just let yourself 'be' the big wall of fat. What kinds of qualities does it have?"

Jen sighed heavily, then she was quiet for a moment. When she spoke again, her voice was somber. "It's thick and solid."

"And if this thick, solid fat could 'talk,' what would it be saying?"

She paused. Then in a brusque voice, she said, "You're not going to push me around!"

When I asked how old the voice was, Jen was surprised to find it was 'thirteen years old.'

"And is this thirteen-year-old standing anywhere in particular?"

"I'm in the kitchen. My mom's laying into me about some stupid thing—telling me that I don't do enough around the house, or what a selfish daughter I am...and my dad's just standing behind her, agreeing with her."

"So, your mom's laying into you, and your 'fat' is a big solid wall saying, 'You're not going to push me around!'"

Jen's face lit up with the insight. "That's how I stood my ground with them! The fat was a 'wall' so they couldn't squash me with their bitching!" She sat up a little taller. "I didn't know it was a protection... Wow, that's a different story. Maybe my fat isn't the enemy."

I smiled, happy that she saw the connection. "I think your fat has been your ally."

Our Body, Our Great Ally

Our body may be a vehicle for our aliveness, but it is also a great communicator. Through our postures, facial expressions, and the tension we hold in our body, as well as the weight and musculature of our body, we convey our beliefs, values, emotions, and fears. Jen had been ignoring her body for years, convinced that her fat was worthless, but when she mindfully turned toward it, it offered her potent information. The very thing Jen disdained about her body had, in fact, been protecting her: *You're not going to push me around!*

The mental formations we carry inside are explicitly expressed in our body. If we believe that the world is an unsafe place, our body can assume tough postures or extra weight in order to protect us; we may develop a strong body with braced muscles or walk around with a scowl on our face. If we carry a lonely child within, we may stare at the ground with a sad expression, rarely expecting anyone to engage us. If we carry a scared, anxious child within, we may startle easily, and our movements may be jerky and reactive.

Mental formations are also entwined with our illnesses, injuries, eating disorders, addictions, and chronic pain. For example, if we struggle with an eating disorder, there may be a formation that hollers, *Food is bad!* or *I have to eat! I'm starving!* If we struggle with addictions, we may hear a voice inside us panicking. *I can't handle this! I need the pain to stop!* If we have been injured, we may have a formation that is still living out the accident. *I'm scared! I'm scared! I'm scared!* How do mental formations get intwined with physical expression? The answer lies in the symbiotic relationship between our mind and body.

The Mind/Body Connection

The human body is quite amazing. The moment our body experiences sights, sounds, sensations, and scents, our mind instantly interprets them, "That's apple pie!" "That's beautiful!" "That hurts!" The same happens even if we *think* about an object: If we call up a memory of warm apple pie, we may smile as our body relaxes in pleasure. If we think about a scary movie, our body may cringe or brace in fear. How does this occur?

Within our body, billions of brain cells are interwoven with our muscles, joints, organs, and skin, creating an instant link between our muscles, organs, and our brain. This mind/body connection is vital for our survival—if we hear an animal charging us, a flash of movement can save our life. Commonly referred to as the *fight-flight/fawn-freeze response*, these mind/body instincts kick into protection mode anytime we encounter fear or trauma. The mind/body connection also gifts us in other ways, for it enlivens our human experience: the neurons wired throughout our body produce an experience of feeling truly *alive*. The neurons wrapped around our heart give us the impression that our heart feels "happy" or "sad." The neurons in our digestive system give us a "gut reaction" where our body seemingly "knows" when something is off. Similarly, if you've ever had a headache during a stressful meeting, felt nauseous before an unpleasant experience, or felt a "flutter" in your heart when that special someone walks into the room, you've experienced the mind/body connection at work.

> With this mind/body connection, we can "listen" to our body to pick up clues about our inner experience.

This mind/body phenomenon is so common, our language is packed with references to it. When we are happy, we might say, "My heart is overjoyed!" When we are sad, "My heart sank," or "My heart is heavy." When we are distressed, we may whine, "I feel sick to my stomach," or describing our fear, we may say, "My blood ran cold." When we are stressed, we might grumble, "My stomach is tied up in knots," or "My head's about to explode!" These idioms exemplify the entwinement of our mind and body acting as one organism, expressing our human experience.

With this mind/body connection, we can "listen" to our body to pick up clues about our inner experience. Feeling our stomach contract, we may realize that we are scared. Noticing that our jaw is tight, we can recognize that we are stressed. If we deepen into these sensations, we discover that they are doorways to our inner world—contractions, bracing, excitement, and agitation, point to emotional aspects of our experience. Asking a "ball of fire" or a "wall of fat" to *talk*, we elicit a voice from our past—a memory from long ago—just as Clarise and Jen found when they asked their body to "talk."

Listening To Your Body

What is your body saying to the world? To get a clearer sense of this, you can try this experiment: Stand with your eyes closed and allow your body to take on its familiar stance and posture. Notice how you hold your body. Are there any places where you hold tension or stress? For example, is your jaw set tight or is your back braced? Notice your posture and musculature—do you stand tall, with sharp and defined muscles, or is your body soft and slouching? Are you relaxed and at ease, or are you standing ready for a fight or an attack?

If this body could talk, what would it be saying to the world? *I'm awesome... I love being alive... I can handle myself... I'm strong!* Or perhaps, it says, *Leave me alone! Back off!* Maybe it's saying, *I'm sad... lonely...depressed...scared.* Our body is always conveying our inner world. If you are struggling with your body or what your body is saying, I invite you to offer yourself some Loving Kindness right here in this moment, offering compassionate kindness to the body you have. We all deserve tender care when our body is suffering.

This mind/body connection is our great ally as it points directly to the formations and memories that need attention and release. When our mind/body awareness is paired with Essence and our soothing practices, we have a safe, effective means for healing our wounds and releasing our limiting beliefs: Our body reveals the memories that are blocking our aliveness and growth, soothing practices release our anxiety and tension, and Essence calms us, confirming that at our deepest level we are safe and unharmed by the pains we have encountered in life. With these resources, we have the means to pinpoint and resolve any pain or limiting narrative that hinders our growth and development.

With the release of our formations, we heal both our mind and body. As "earlier me" leaves the body, its fearful mind-state dissipates, our mind relaxes, and our body comes into ease, just as Clarise did when she released her little kindergartener—as the energy released out of her body, she settled and relaxed. Through release work, our body is transformed, settling into its more natural alignment—pain disappears, tightness softens, our shoulders drop, and our breathing grows quiet and steady. With ongoing release work, over time we can see significant physical transformation, awakening a healthier, more adaptive body.

This brings us to an important point. If our body mirrors our internal beliefs and fears, it may be difficult to come into full physical healing while our mind is holding onto painful beliefs and narratives. If our fat plays a protective role (as it did for Jen), it may be hard to lose weight. If we are flooded with angry formations, our face always held in a scowl, it may be hard to resolve our TMJ disorder (tight jaw). If we carry a depressed inner child within us, we may struggle to find the energy to eat or exercise, compromising our overall health and well-being.

You may see the truth of this in your own life. How often have you tried to change a physical habit only to regress back to old patterns? This scenario is so common people joke about how quickly they will abandon their New Year's resolutions. We may lose weight, only to gain it back. We may start exercising and give it up a week later. We may try to quit smoking or drinking and find ourselves reaching for our addictive crutch in a moment of stress.

If we want to create strong physical health and vitality, it benefits us greatly to release the psychological stories and formations that are entwined with our physical maladies. With an injury, we can augment our healing when we release the fears, memories, and beliefs associated with that injury. If we are having surgery, we can release any fear or pain related to the surgery. If we are struggling with illness, we can support our healing by bubbling out the stressful fears and negative beliefs related to our illness. In my experience, those who practice release work around their physical maladies often report shorter healing times, less pain and fatigue, deeper resting, and in some cases, a resolution of their affliction.

As I stated earlier, intense chronic pain tends to hold larger, more painful stories. If you are dealing with significant physical challenges and wish to work with the formations involved, it can benefit you greatly to engage a healer who is skilled in somatic release therapy. Somatic release work refers to any healing therapies that aid in releasing pain, fear, or trauma from the body. However, as you develop a strong release practice and strengthen your connection with Essence, in time, you can work with deeper afflictions on your own.

A New Way of Being

If Jen was going to create a healthier life, she needed to clear the belief that her fat was her protector. Giving up food as her comfort and shield would require a reliable source of deep inner support and nourishment that could keep her safe and grounded in her life. What was this source? Her own Essence.

As Jen rested on the couch noticing the thirteen-year-old, I brought her attention back to her Essence. "So, take a moment to notice the quiet in the background."

Jen wrinkled her nose. "I don't sense a quiet. It feels more like space—a big open space."

"Okay, go with that! There's lots of ways to experience our deeper nature. You can let yourself breathe into that open space."

"Now, as you're resting in this open spaciousness, what two qualities are present?"

With her eyes closed, Jen murmured, "I feel expansive and calm."

"Great. So, as you're resting this expansive calm, allow Essence to access this memory. Your mother's yelling at you, and Essence is standing there, expansive and calm, watching her. Notice something... Does Essence feel thirteen?" Jen shook her head.

"Is it yelling, 'Don't push me around?'"

"No, it's really peaceful. It's just watching her. It's not bothered at all; it's like her anger can't reach me."

Softly, I said, "This feeling of 'distance' you're describing with Essence allows us to feel safe, as if the drama is 'over there,' far away from us. So, as you're calmly watching your mother and father as they're berating you, what does Essence notice? What's really going on with them over there?"

Jen was quiet for a moment. Then in a soft voice, full of clarity, she said, "My mom's scared that she can't control me. She controls my dad, but she can't control me. She keeps picking on me hoping to break me down." She let out a long exhale. "They're not really grown-ups, they're more like adolescents. That's why they use drugs all the time; they can't handle their life." Anchored in Essence, Jen was getting a new perspective—a new story—about herself and her parents. She was experiencing a clarity, strength and composure she hadn't known before.

"And as Essence sees your parents in their fear and adolescent orientation, how does it want to relate to them?"

Jen was clear and confident: "I feel compassion for them, but I know they're not going to 'show up' as parents for me."

"And if they don't 'show up' as parents for you, is Essence worried about that?"

Jen cracked a faint smile. "No, I'm fine. I can take care of myself."

Now that she saw the bigger picture about her parents and she knew she would be "fine," I invited Jen's thirteen-year-old to release. In typical teen fashion, the girl chose to go hang out with some friends.

As the formation began to release, Jen's body shook with a slight tremor. "So, what are you noticing right now?"

Jen sighed. "I notice that I'm shaking, and there's a lot of heat leaving my belly. I think it's coming from the fat."

Reassuring her, I softly said, "That 'shaking' that you're noticing is just the energy of the formation leaving the body. It's totally normal—sometimes, our body just shakes. Just relax...let the body shake and let the heat rise out of the fat... If it feels intense, you can always step back into Essence and watch the energy dissipate as you rest in Essence."

Jen exhaled and sank back into the couch. "Actually, it feels good. It's kinda comforting."

"I'm glad it feels good. So as this energy's leaving, I'd like you to notice... Are you shrinking or fading?"

"No, I feel bigger...stronger...more energy." Jen's sense of protection was now coming from her Essence, not her physical weight.

* * *

When Jen released her fear and pain, I wasn't surprised that her body tremored or she felt heat rising from her belly, as it's all part of the mind/body connection. Anytime we feel threatened or under attack, our body tenses as part of the fight-flight-freeze response. As formations form, the intense energy of the fearful moment gets frozen in our body—we are frozen in a scream, frozen in bracing, frozen in a protective move such as shielding our face with our hands. As we release the formation, all the energy bound up in that formation leaves the body through tingling or bubbling out, shaking, tremors, heat rising or pressure releasing. This makes sense, as the energy has to go *somewhere*.

The "bracing" and "holding" of energy in our body points to an interesting phenomenon. As part of the fight-flight-freeze response, whenever we are scared, energy is diverted away from our digestive system to our extremities in order to support quick movement—a great survival mechanism. But this survival reflex can leave us feeling bloated and heavy when we are stressed, for our digestion stops during stressful moments.

Consequently, when we release our stress, pain, or trauma, our vagus nerve relaxes, cueing our body that it's safe to go back to digestion—our belly softens, and any stored energy is released, often as heat. So, it was quite normal for Jen to feel heat rising out of her belly as she relaxed and her digestive system came back into alignment. Beyond the release of heat, it is also normal for people to shake, tremor, and sometimes, even fart—which feels awesome when you've been feeling bloated! As I said earlier, the more we release tension from our body, the more we begin to feel like our natural selves.

After several more release sessions, Jen decided to call her parents to talk about their substance abuse and its impact on their relationship. Not surprisingly, she didn't get very far. Her mother reacted harshly, calling her a "selfish, ungrateful daughter" and her father sided with her mother, saying that Jen was "making a mountain out of a molehill."

"What was that like for you?" I asked when she told me about the exchange.

She gave a tired smile and leaned back into the couch. "I would have been undone by them in the past. But as they were ranting, I remembered to step back into Essence. As I rested in Essence, listening to them, I could see their pain so clearly; how stuck they are in their fear and substance abuse. After I hung up, I laid on the floor and let all the sadness and hurt rise out of my body, just like we do in here. I cried a little—I had a little girl inside who wanted parents who would care for her, but I released her. She went off to be with nice, sober parents. Afterwards, I felt much lighter and...*free*."

I smiled warmly. "I'm glad you're feeling 'free.' When we connect with our Essence and release our pain and stress as it comes up, we don't create any new formations—the pain arises and passes away, and with that flow of energy, our mind and body stay open and free."

Jen smiled. "That's a lot better than storing it in my body. The more I release, the lighter I feel, even though it's not going well with my parents. I wish it was different with them, but they're not going to change anytime soon. If I want a happy life, I guess I'll have to do it myself."

As Jen found, releasing stress "on the spot" and grounding in Essence anchors us in a clarity and strength that keeps us light and free, even when we are dealing with stressful situations. These practices demonstrate that it is not the "outside conditions" that make us safe and relaxed, but the "inside conditions" that determine our well-being.

> It is not the "outside conditions" that make us safe and relaxed, but the "inside conditions" that determine our well-being.

We can find great benefit in releasing our accumulated stress each day. After a difficult day at work, you can take ten–fifteen minutes to release your stress before you go home. If you work at home, consider doing some release work before engaging with your family. To do this, find a comfortable position (you can even lie on the floor with a cushion under your knees), and close your eyes. Breathing out the tension or stress from your day, notice any tightness in your body and imagine the tightness as energy, allowing it to "bubble" out of your body. When you are finished releasing, take some time to rest in Essence. If you walk home from work, you might take ten minutes to sit in a beautiful spot and let the tension rise out of your body before you go home. If you have experienced a lot of stress, you might notice your body trembling or shaking as the tension releases. This is totally normal. Just allow the trembling and rest calmly in Essence or imagine yourself resting in a big, natural space. After you've let off some stress, rest in the supports around you: Let the park bench 'hold' you...listen to the bird songs...relish the sounds of the city or children playing...all while resting in Essence.

We can also bring these practices into stressful events. During a medical procedure, you can release your tension and stress as the procedure unfolds. Close your eyes and imagine your fear or tension bubbling out of your body as you rest in Essence. You might also remind yourself that this procedure is an act of love or care meant to heal you. You can also say some Loving Kindness for yourself as the procedure unfolds. With these practices, we can release fear and tension in any stressful moment—during a family argument, while you are worrying about loved ones, or when you are waiting for test results. The more we learn to release our stress and tension and rest in Essence, the more we stay centered and relaxed, creating the best conditions for our overall health and well-being.

Importantly, we can offer these practices to children as well. Anytime a child is hurt or scared, you can invite them to let the "owie" or the "scary part" bubble out of their body, up to the sky, imagining the bubbles going *up, up, up.* Children are naturals at release as they live in an imaginative world. Importantly, make sure that you also tell the child that the scary thing is "all finished." By doing this, we cue their mind and body to know that the trauma has ended: "You're not falling anymore." "The doggie isn't biting you anymore." "It's all over." "The [scary thing] is all gone!" When children release their fear and pain on the spot, they remain open and free, and they are much less likely to form overwhelmed formations in their mind and body.

Cultivating Our Physical Well-being

With the release of our limiting fears and beliefs, we are ready for the next step in our healing: Learning new skills and developing our potential. In the Physical Domain, this means cultivating our physical capacity for the most aliveness and freedom. We may decide to get in shape or take up a new sport—it could be running or pickleball. We might commit to walking or running with a friend several times a week. Or we may take up activities that foster our self-expression—we might go dancing, take an art class, sign up for singing lessons, or take up a musical instrument. We might even make a vow to ourselves to become more playful, saying "Yes!" whenever we are invited to physical outings such as hiking, bike riding, or camping. And importantly, we can explore how our Essence *moves* through our body.

As Jen continued her release work, at home and in our sessions, she was no longer reaching for Bing Cherry Madness for comfort and relief.

Instead, she was becoming more interested in her own self-care. She started going for walks after school each day and she was consciously trying to eat healthier. Then on a warm summer day, she bounced into my office with a big smile on her face.

"Guess what? I've decided to take dance classes! I've always wanted to dance. To me, dancing is pure freedom and joy. There's a set of classes starting in the fall and…" She deflated, as if all the air had gone out of her dream, and frowned.

"What's the matter?" I asked.

"What if I'm too big to be in the class? What if I look stupid?" Suddenly, she looked like a scared, self-conscious child.

I wasn't surprised these fears were coming up. Whenever we step into new, uncharted territory, we are often bombarded with past memories and formations from when we were inexperienced or awkward.

I smiled warmly. "Would you like to release those fears? I bet if you let them go, you'll do just fine in the class!"

Jen looked up brightly. "Oh, these are formations! I didn't realize that! I just feel all this scared energy running through my body. Yes, let's release them!"

As we tracked down the fearful voices, they showed themselves to be holdouts from when Jen first gained weight as a teenager, and she got teased about it. With the release of her formations, Jen settled into Essence, smiling.

"So, what comes up when Essence considers taking a dance class?"

She smiled brightly. "Essence is excited to dance! It's gonna be fun!"

As she was getting up to leave that day, I offered a light suggestion. "Jen, whenever you try something new, it helps to let go of thinking about it and just let Essence play. If you're going to dance, just dance! *Don't think, just dance.* If you're riding a bike, just ride. Don't think about how you look riding the bike, or whether you're going to fall. When we stop thinking and simply *live* through our bodies, we're transformed—there is just *dancing... running...making love.* And as we get swept up in the aliveness, we open to our True Nature. It feels fun to just play and enjoy being alive!"

Jen grinned. "That's so funny! That's exactly what I tell my students about science: 'Just jump in and have fun! Don't think about it; just experiment, make mistakes, have a blast!' You know, *fun* and *freedom* is what births little scientists!" She smiled. "I guess the same holds true for dancers! Okay, I'll sign up for the class today." She threw me a mischievous grin. "Who knows, I might even wear my tutu to class one day!"

Cultivating Your Physical Well-being

What physical adventures call to you? What pleasant experiences soothe and nourish your body—going for a hike, taking a nice warm bath, walking in a park, going for a run? Perhaps you enjoy riding your bike, camping with your kids, or taking your dog for a walk. Maybe you would like to take up Zumba or rock climbing.

Next time you engage in a physical activity, take a moment to land in the joy and the nourishment of the movement. Don't think, just *do* it. Notice how it feels when you *enjoy* the activity. As you fill with joy and aliveness in your play, take a moment to breathe the delight through your whole being. When you let go into physical joy, you are rewiring your body and mind for greater health and well-being.

Over the next year, Jen continued to release her painful narratives and she danced to her heart's content. As she did this, Jen's body began to heal. She lost fifty pounds, her blood pressure stabilized, and importantly, she landed in her natural body—she had more "flow" in her movements, she walked taller, and she fully expressed her beautiful spirit in her physical presence. Jen's healing wasn't about her body size; for many people embody flow, joy, and aliveness in all kinds of bodies—large bodies, small bodies, queer bodies, athletic bodies, and physically challenged bodies. The key is whether we are embodying freedom, joy, and well-being in our physical expression. When we come home to our True Nature in the Physical Domain, we express the healthiest body possible.

True Success in the Physical Domain has many expressions. It is a woman in her nineties who loves dancing. It is the mom who runs with her baby in a stroller. And it is my friend Jayce who, after his stroke, exercises every day to keep his body active and agile. It is the entrepreneur who invites communities to help him build gardens in their urban landscapes. It is your friend, going through chemotherapy, who gets out to walk on *most* days. It is the high school athlete practicing endless hours, so she can earn a place on a college team. And it is the parents who trade off the kids, so each of them can get some time to exercise.

> Whatever body you have, you have the potential to open its aliveness and bring it home to Essence.

Whatever body you have, you have the potential to open its aliveness and bring it home to Essence. Even if you contend with physical difficulties, turn toward your body with kindness and attention, and it will reveal its secrets and its passions, opening the way to more aliveness and vitality. When you take up residence in the physical wing of your castle, you awaken the presence of a loved body and the gifts of a truly successful, embodied life.

The Cognitive Domain
The Freedom to Be a Lifelong Learner

When you awoke this morning, what was your routine? Perhaps you looked at your phone or clock to see what time it was... checked your texts or messages...got out of bed...got dressed...talked to your partner, your pet, or yourself...made some breakfast...checked the weather...thought about your tasks for the day...then turned on your computer or left for work. However your morning unfolded, you can thank your Cognitive Domain, for none of it could have happened without it.

The Cognitive Domain is where rational thinking, processing, and learning takes place. The term "cognition" comes from the Latin word *cognitus*, meaning "getting to know or acquire knowledge of," and it is often associated with academic pursuits such as reading, writing, and math, but cognition encompasses far more than that. Specifically, it refers to the mental processes that are involved in logical thinking, learning, remembering, and performing tasks. While the Psychological and Cognitive Domains both involve mental thinking, they hold different functions: The Psychological Domain is where we use thinking to create meanings, beliefs, stories, and values; the Cognitive Domain encompasses the mental "steps" of thinking and processing that allows us to create beliefs and do any activity. In truth, we cannot cross a street, drive a car, write an email, cook a meal, or organize our day without thinking and mental processing, which makes the Cognitive Domain vital for successful living. On the road to True Success, we might say that the Cognitive Domain is the "brains behind the wheel."

Cognition encompasses three operations: We *take in* information through our senses, *process* that information in order to understand and work with it, then *respond* in line with our processing. For example, we may be walking in a park when suddenly we catch a whiff of something. Breathing in the scent, we process the information, trying to place it— *it's sweet...pungent...earthy...*our mind runs through a list of possible fragrances. *Oh, it's lavender!* Once it's identified, we respond. If we love lavender, we may eagerly seek out the plant and bend down to inhale its sweet fragrance, nourished by its scent. If we dislike the scent of lavender or have bad memories associated with it, we may pull back, "Ewww!" and quickly walk away. These cognitive faculties—intake, process, and response—work together to help us make sense of the world and respond accordingly.

Difficulties arise in the Cognitive Domain when any of these three operations are challenged or compromised. For example, if you struggle with sensory input—perhaps you don't see or hear clearly—you may take in information inaccurately, leading to mistaken conclusions about your experience. If you have difficulty with thinking and processing— you struggle to understand concepts or cannot retain what you have learned—you may be unable to utilize the information you receive. If you struggle with self-expression—you have a speech impediment or have trouble writing—you may have difficulty conveying your thoughts and ideas to others; for example, you may hear a poem and are moved by its depth yet stumble as you try to describe your insights to others.

Cognitive limitations can arise from any number of factors. Some of us are born with learning challenges that impact our cognitive processing. Other times, sickness, injury, exhaustion, hunger, or intoxication can affect our ability to think and process clearly. Our thinking may also be impaired by emotional factors. When we are depressed, grieving, overly excited, or anxious, it's hard to focus and process information; we've all experienced moments of fear when we couldn't think straight or figure out what to do next.

When we are struggling with cognitive difficulties, it is important to address these conditions; otherwise, success may elude us. Once we identify the root of our cognitive issues, we can bring in supports to improve our brain's functioning. Some difficulties may require long-term interventions, such as tutoring, neurofeedback, medication, or testing accommodations to help us be more successful. Other cognitive breakdowns are temporary, remedied with lifestyle changes such as eating a snack or getting a good night's sleep. When we take care of our brain, our brain takes care of us, empowering us to achieve our dreams and goals.

> When we take care of our brain, our brain takes care of us, empowering us to achieve our dreams and goals.

As we aim for a more successful life, it can be helpful to understand the functions that support healthy cognitive processing. With this information, we can have a better sense of our strengths and weaknesses and know which areas to target if we are struggling with thinking and processing. Below are some primary faculties that support cognitive success. As you read through them, you might note for yourself which of these functions are effortless for you and which ones need support or cultivation.

Attention allows us to hold our focus on information, objects, and present-moment experience. If we struggle with attention—if our mind is distractable or "jumps around," we may be unable to concentrate on instructions or complete our tasks. With sustained attention, we can stay engaged with our projects to achieve our goals.

Perception interprets information that we take in through our senses (seeing, hearing, etc.). For example, we may see a shape and instantly perceive that it is a cat, or we hear the terse tone in our mother's voice and recognize that her tone implies "irritation." If we misperceive what we are seeing or hearing—let's say that cat turns out to be a skunk, or we misinterpret the tone in our mother's voice and assume she's joking—that misunderstanding can disrupt our entire day. Accurate perceptions empower us to make proper sense of the world, helping us make healthy choices.

Memory allows us to store information so we can draw upon it to inform our present-moment experience. *Long-term memory* preserves details from our past so we don't have to relearn every day how to dress ourselves, drive a car, get to work, do our job, or buy a coffee at the café. It also ensures that we remember our family members and relevant information about them, such as the date of their birthday. *Short-term working memory* keeps new and current information readily available as we work on projects and organize our day. It enables us to keep a to-do list in our head, manage details in our job, hold figures in our head as we do math calculations, and remember to turn off the lights when we leave a room. Success in any venture requires both long-term and short-term memory to get things done.

Executive Functioning allows us to organize information and tasks in an efficient way to achieve our goals. If we are organizing a project or our to-do list, we need to know how to prioritize information: what is important to consider, what can be put aside, and which tasks to do first, second, third, etc. For instance, if you are making dinner for friends and need to pick up some groceries, it doesn't work well to go to the store, come home, then go out to the bank, then go back to the store because you forgot something. Well-developed executive functioning allows us to execute the steps of our goals effectively.

Auditory Processing involves hearing and interpreting sound. It allows us to enjoy music, birdsongs, and the sound of a babbling brook, as well as follow conversations, understand a podcast, and grasp directions when someone describes how to get to a destination. If you struggle to understand what people are saying, or need to write things down when others give you verbal instructions, you may be struggling with auditory processing, missing information that could help you thrive. Hearing, listening, and understanding are key skills in creating successful outcomes in any arena.

Visual Processing involves taking in and interpreting visual information so we can navigate our environment. It also allows us to process information received through reading, watching media, and observing the world. If we cannot see well or struggle with conditions such as dyslexia, we may miss visual information that can help us work effectively. When we clearly see the world, we are much more likely to be successful in what we set out to do.

Expressive Processing allows us to share our ideas, thoughts, and feelings through talking, writing, gestures, or art. It is hard to feel successful if we cannot share our inner world or convey our thoughts and experiences. If we struggle to communicate, others may even perceive our awkwardness as a lack of intelligence. The ability to clearly articulate our thoughts and ideas helps us be successful in social encounters and advancing our visions.

Thinking is a multi-faceted faculty using various processes to understand and work with ideas, information, and meanings in our world.

Analytical thinking breaks down complex ideas and structures into smaller parts so we can understand how the parts work together to create functional whole systems. We use analytical thinking when we are fixing a car, figuring out how to spell a word, organizing a project, or writing computer code.

Abstract thinking is the ability to hold conceptual ideas and information in our mind as we work to solve problems, invent solutions, strategize new directions, and envision creative projects such as planning a trip to Mars. Abstract thinking also allows us to grasp visionary concepts such as "love," "truth," "beauty," "justice," and "racism," as well as philosophical ideas and spiritual beliefs. We also use this faculty when imagining what people mean when they speak indirectly about a concept or situation, such as when someone uses the expression, "The Big C" to mean *cancer*.

Visual-spatial thinking sees patterns and connections in our visual field, allowing us to navigate and use space effectively. We use this faculty when mapping a route, parking a car, aiming a dart at a dartboard, arranging a room, strategizing a sports play, or packing a suitcase.

Social thinking interprets facial expressions, social cues, and tone of voice in order to effectively interact with others. Being able to accurately "read the room" allows us to engage with others in ways that are appropriate and constructive.

Our proficiency in these mental processes determines how successful we will be in any situation. With good social thinking skills, we can easily relate with others, recognize when social interactions are "off," and instinctively know how to repair them. When we are gifted in visual-spatial thinking, we "see" the best way to run a soccer ball up the field to outmaneuver the other team or aim our kick with precision to score a goal. When we are gifted in executive functioning, we use our organizing brilliance to set goals, run projects, and solve problems, whether it's planning our vacation, doing home repairs, or checking off our to-do list at work. With effective thinking, processing, and action, we can be successful in all areas of our life. If we find that we are struggling in any of these areas, we can always develop these mental processes for better functioning.

No one person is gifted in *all* the functions of the Cognitive Domain. Given our strengths and weaknesses, along with our cultivation, we each have different Lines of Development—we are skillful in some areas and struggle in others. A brilliant professor may teach doctoral level courses yet have a hard time organizing her files. A college applicant may get a 1500 on his SAT and write computer code, yet he can't figure out how to parallel park his car. A gifted surgeon may perform miracles in the operating room yet have terrible social skills and struggle to understand his patients' emotional needs. A talented musician may be able to pick out a line in a song and play it on multiple instruments yet be unable to read music. In the Cognitive Domain, all of us have a "mixed" profile; in some areas we are gifted, in others, we are disorganized.

As you reflect on your Cognitive Domain, in what areas do you shine? Perhaps you love working with math, science, or technology. You may love reading, or you have been told that you are a talented writer. Perhaps you enjoy managing projects and solving problems. Maybe you excel at a favorite hobby—you're great at building things, videogaming, quilting, or doing crossword puzzles. As you reflect on the areas where you feel "smart"—the places where your thinking and processing are sharp and efficient—how do these capacities contribute to your success in life?

Are there ways in which you struggle cognitively? Perhaps math or reading have never been easy. Maybe your plans, ideas, and projects are always in chaos. Perhaps you have a short attention span, or it's hard to remember names or details. You may contend with autism or struggle in social situations—it's hard for you to "read" people or understand what's going on in social groups. Perhaps your mind is not as sharp as it once was. As you reflect on the thinking processes where you struggle, how have these difficulties impacted your efforts to live a successful life?

If cognitive difficulties are hampering your efforts to live successfully, know that it's possible to develop and strengthen our faculties, even as adults, for our brain can grow and develop throughout our life. Through a process of *neuroplasticity*, our brain can build new neural networks in response to new learning and engagement with the world, well into our later years. As it turns out, an old dog can learn new tricks! With neuroplasticity, we can overcome learning challenges, develop new coping strategies, and figure out how to work our smartphone after it downloads a new update! Through the magic of neuroplasticity, we can become *lifelong learners*, able to create ongoing success throughout our life.

The Cognitive Domain is vital in creating True Success for it powers every domain. Our Physical Domain requires thinking, coordination, and memory to pull off our physical feats. Our Psychological and Emotional Domains need memory, sensory processing, and communication skills to thrive. Our Social-Relational Domain requires attention, perception, and social thinking to flourish. In True Success, we recognize that the

Cognitive Domain is the "brains" that drives our life in a desired direction, so we aim to create the best possible conditions for cognitive fitness.

Engaging New Learning

Is there something new that you would like to learn? Perhaps you would like to take a class in astronomy, study a foreign language, learn how to code, or develop your leadership skills. Maybe you would like to join a book club or an online discussion group on your favorite topic. I invite you to take a leap and engage in some fun learning opportunities. New learning will not only sharpen your mind, but it will open a door to a more interesting, satisfying life. The skills you develop through new learning can also help you achieve your dreams and aspirations.

Cognitive Stories That Limit Us

On a hot summer day, Ryan, the jovial wilderness guide, barreled into my office and vaulted himself onto the couch. He had just returned from a river trip and was sporting the windswept look of someone who'd spent a week outdoors, but instead of looking renewed and enlivened, he was clearly agitated. Sitting on the edge of the couch, his leg jiggled frenetically.

"What's wrong?" I asked.

"What's wrong?! I'll tell you what's wrong... This thing with my boss just gets worse! I'm just a guide, but he's on me like I'm a manager!"

"Well, you did say that Steve wants you to take over the business and that he thinks of you as a son... Perhaps he's just grooming his 'successor.'"

"Yeah, well, 'Dad' just yelled at me for not turning in a report on my last trip. He called me 'incompetent!' Can you believe that?! He can't do *half* of what I do out there! So what, if I missed a stupid report! You know what this is?! It's that stupid Cognitive Domain! I HATE math and reading; it takes too long to do the reports, and I've got other stuff to do!" Ryan glanced out the window and sighed, exasperated. With his exhalation, all the agitation drained out of him, and he slumped over, rubbing his forehead as he stared at the floor. "I don't know what I was thinking... I'm too stupid to take this management job." He buried his face in his hands. "Ugh! I feel like I'm going to throw up."

Gently, I said, "Let's take a moment to settle, then we can look at this. Why don't you close your eyes and take a few breaths..." Ryan closed his eyes, letting out a few shaky breaths. "Now, imagine that you're outside in a big, beautiful natural space—it might be a river valley...a meadow... on top of a mountain...or a beach...some place relaxing, with a nice big sky. As you sit in this big open space, breathe out your tension and let all the stress and anxiety rise off, up into the open sky. Give this stressful energy lots of room."

I waited as Ryan's breathing slowed and his body relaxed. With his eyes still closed, he nodded. "This is better."

"I'm glad you feel better. Anytime we have big energy or big feelings in our body, it helps to give it *lots* of room. Imagining a wide, calming space allows the energy to dissipate, giving us room to feel safe and relaxed."

Ryan opened his eyes and sat up, looking a bit more relieved. "I imagined that I was sitting in a big open valley with a wide river. It felt great!"

I smiled, happy that he felt relieved. "I'm glad that was helpful. Anytime we experience big energy, whether it's from anxiety, rage, dizziness, or nausea, it can feel pretty overwhelming, for the energy in our body works a lot like flowing water: If we have a lot of it moving through us and we're contracted, it feels like water rushing through a tight space, such as a slot canyon; it rises up fifteen feet and we feel like we're drowning. But if we open that narrow canyon into a big river valley, the water level drops and spreads out: Same amount of water, but now we're walking through calm, peaceful shallows."

"When you were braced against the shame and distress you felt about being 'stupid,' you contracted, creating the slot canyon, and that made the shameful energy feel overwhelming and nauseating. By imagining a big river valley, you relaxed into spaciousness, allowing the stressful energy to flow and dissipate. Same amount of energy, you just gave it room to discharge."

Ryan smiled faintly. "It was definitely easier when I imagined the river valley. I felt like I could breathe."

"Well now that you're settled, let's go back to what upset you—that Steve said you were incompetent, and you felt stupid. When you were swirling in those labels, you forgot that he admires and trusts you... that he respects your leadership skills...and you forgot all about your Essence."

Ryan glanced down at the floor. "Yeah... I can handle a lot of things—boats flipping, rescues in the backcountry, screaming tourists tied to a cliff—but if somebody treats me like I'm stupid, that sends me over the edge."

"Yes, but *you* said that you were stupid. So somewhere inside you must believe that, otherwise, people's opinions about your intelligence wouldn't bother you. I'm curious about where you got this idea that you're 'stupid.'"

Ryan frowned. "Maybe I *am* stupid. I was always bad at school." Suddenly, he looked like a lost boy, all his charisma and confidence swallowed up by a story from his past. No wonder it was hard for him to imagine himself in a manager's role.

"It sounds like you made a decision about yourself long ago that is getting in your way now. I imagine there's a good reason why you struggle with math and reading, but clearly you are not 'stupid,' Ryan. It takes a lot of brains to do what you do as a wilderness guide. There are lots of ways to excel in the Cognitive Domain, and beyond math and reading, you're 'smart' in many areas. Whatever happened in school, doesn't have to define you for the rest of your life."

Ryan nodded, still looking disheartened. "I'd like to believe that," he said softly.

Your Cognitive Story

How do you describe yourself in the Cognitive Domain? Perhaps you think, *I'm smart...stupid...average...an idiot.* Maybe you believe *I'm smarter than most people.* Or you tell yourself, *I stink at math...reading... writing...organizing.* How do these descriptions impact your life? Our psychological beliefs about our "intelligence" often lay out a course that we then follow, supporting or limiting us in our endeavors.

Are there any cognitive labels that you would like to put down? What might be possible if you no longer believe these labels?

What Exactly Is Intelligence?

When we consider our capacities in the Cognitive Domain, we often focus on one question: *Am I smart?* The issue looms large as we often believe that our intelligence is a measure of our worth or value. We may look at others and wonder... *Am I as smart as my brother or sister...my best friend...my coworkers? Am I smart enough for this job?* When we compare our intelligence against that of others, how exactly are we defining "intelligence," and what does this definition say about us?

As we saw earlier, *cognition* refers to the steps of mental processing—taking in information, assessing and interpreting it, and then acting on those interpretations. *Intelligence* is a measure of how easily and effectively we do these steps. We use cognitive processes in all kinds of activities—deep sea fishing, running a company, midwifing a birth, running a farm—and all of these activities require intelligence. But in our western culture, intelligence is typically measured through IQ, an intelligence quotient, which is based on our aptitude in language and math skills. Our society also equates intelligence with academic knowledge, but success in academia is only one area of intelligence. As it turns out, there are many ways to be "smart."

Howard Gardner, a developmental psychologist at Harvard University, has challenged our understanding of intelligence by introducing a new concept—*multiple intelligences.* Dr. Gardner asserts that when language and mathematical abilities are the sole measure of intelligence, we overlook other cognitive capacities that are vital in creating a successful life. The areas of intelligence that Dr. Gardner proposes include:

Linguistic-Verbal Intelligence
reading, writing, and language

Logical/Mathematical Intelligence
working with math, formulas, sequences

Visual-spatial Intelligence
visual acuity, mapping routes, precision work

Musical Intelligence
producing and working with music and sound

Body/Kinesthetic Intelligence
being physically gifted or moving with precision

Interpersonal Intelligence
being gifted at working with people

Intrapersonal Intelligence
knowing your mind and your internal world

Naturalistic Intelligence
decoding and working with nature, plants, animals, weather

As you reflect on this list, you may realize that you are gifted in several of these areas. How does it feel to recognize that your particular gifts are expressions of intelligence? How does this awareness change your story about whether or not you are "smart?"

There are hundreds and hundreds of ways to succeed and many,
many different abilities that will help you get there.
—*Dr. Howard Gardner*

Intelligence is an innate faculty. We all possess a natural intelligence, a capacity to learn, and an ability to use our knowledge and skills in the world. How we express that intelligence is influenced by what we are exposed to in our environment. For example, if we grow up with parents who are astrophysicists, we may know a lot about black holes and distant galaxies. But accumulated knowledge, about black holes or any other topic, is not always a clear sign of intelligence. Accumulating facts is a function of memory and exposure to knowledge. Intelligence points to our capacity to understand and organize that knowledge in order to navigate our world. It is our ability to work with and manipulate information that creates successful outcomes and shows how intelligent we are. As one elementary teacher told me, "I love teaching third grade because that's where you see children's natural intelligence shine through. Before that, kids can look smart if they've been exposed to a lot of knowledge—maybe their parents traveled with them, or they got lots of instruction and tutoring. But in third grade, we give them schoolwork that doesn't rely on accumulated knowledge. They have to use their own intelligence to respond to something that's new for all of them. It's an absolute joy to watch their natural intelligence sparkle!"

In Dr. Gardner's model, intelligence can be expressed in different domains, any of which can be used to secure success and a meaningful life. Ryan may struggle with Linguistic and Mathematical skills, but he is cognitively brilliant in Body/Kinesthetic, Interpersonal, and Naturalistic intelligences. This is why he is so successful as a wilderness guide: He is able to assess changes in weather and river conditions, knows how to work with scared tourists, he can intuit how to safely guide a raft through Class V rapids, and he can effectively coordinate rescue missions. But if Ryan wanted to manage Mountains and Rivers, he needed to open himself to new learning in math and language skills. If he could release his story that he was "stupid" and take up new learning, he could foster a new identity, one where he could imagine himself as a successful manager and step into that role with confidence.

As we aspire to develop new areas of our own life, there will be many times when we'll be called upon to develop new cognitive capacities to realize our dreams and ambitions. It may take a lot of sweat and work, but we can always get "smarter."

Seeing Beyond Our Labels

Revealing the trouble he'd had in school was a turning point for Ryan, as his belief about being "stupid" was sabotaging his dream of becoming a manager. If we could discover the root of that belief and release it, he could free himself from this painful narrative and open to the supports and cultivation he would need to step into the manager's role. As I watched him staring at his hands, fiddling with a broken nail, I felt such compassion for him. Tenderly, I asked, "So when you said that you were 'bad' at school, did you mean reading, writing, and math?

"Yeah... All of them I guess."

"Was there anything you liked about school?"

Ryan smiled weakly. "P.E. and recess."

I smiled. "That makes sense since you're gifted in physical expression and social interaction."

Ryan perked up with a look of surprise. "I never thought about it that way. That's cool. I guess I am good at *some* domains."

"Actually, you're even 'good' in the Cognitive Domain, you just have varying strengths and weaknesses. Would it be okay if we worked with the school difficulties?"

He sighed. "Yeah, I guess."

"Go ahead and close your eyes and let's get mindful..." Ryan sat back on the couch and closed his eyes. "Now, let yourself remember what it was like to be in school. Just notice what comes up in your mind and body as you reflect on being in school."

"I hated school."

"You said that earlier. Are you making a general statement, or is that what the school kid is saying?"

"That's what I'm saying."

"Okay... But in this exercise, we're using active imagination. So I'd like you to imagine yourself back in school as a kid. What was that like?"

With his eyes shut, Ryan frowned. "I don't like it. I feel kinda panicky, cornered...like I want to get away. And I feel tight all over, like I'm going to explode."

"And if this panic or tightness could talk, what would it be saying?"

He was silent a moment, his brow furrowed. "It feels like it's yelling, 'Leave me alone!'"

"And how old does this voice feel—the one yelling, *Leave me alone!*"

"Fifth grade... Stupid Mrs. McGuire and her dumb book reports! I HATE her! She's such a jerk!!" Ryan had become an angry fifth grader, furious with frustration and annoyance.

"And in this memory are you standing or sitting in a particular place?"

"I'm in front of the class giving the stupid book report. And she's yelling at me in front of everybody! She said I didn't work on it, that I was *incompetent*... But I DID work on it! I worked on it for FIVE DAYS! I tried to read the book and I worked on it every night!"

Angrily, he clutched his stomach. Slowly, he began rocking as a few tears rolled down his face. "What's the point of even trying?! I never get it right anyway."

"I'm sorry she didn't see how hard you worked on your report. That must have been tough, going through that in front of the class."

Ryan nodded as tears fell. "She was so mean!"

I handed him a tissue. "Can you feel that hurt and sadness?" He nodded. "As you're feeling it, you can breathe that hurt and sadness out, you don't have to hold onto it."

After a few shaky breaths, Ryan unfolded his arms and wiped his eyes. Then he leaned back against the couch, resting with his eyes closed. Seeing him calmer, I sensed he was ready to anchor in Essence.

"So as you're feeling this pain, can you also feel your Lifeforce in the background?" Ryan nodded. "Let yourself step back into that quiet energy and breathe into it, letting the peace and ease get as big as it wants." I waited a few moments, then continued. "As you're resting in your Lifeforce, let yourself go back to that classroom... Your Lifeforce is standing in front of the class... Mrs. McGuire is yelling... Now, does your Lifeforce feel like a fifth grader?" Ryan shook his head.

"Is it screaming, 'What's the point of trying?'"

"No. It's calm."

Deepening the exploration, I asked, "As you're standing there, grounded in your Lifeforce in front of the classroom as Mrs. McGuire is saying that you didn't try and you're incompetent...how does your Lifeforce respond?"

Ryan released a long exhale, as a faint smile lit his face. "It's calm. I'm just watching her and I'm okay—even if she says I didn't do it right."

"It sounds like you're having some compassion for yourself."

"Yeah…"

"I'd like you to notice another thing as you're embodying your Lifeforce… Is your Lifeforce 'stupid' or 'incompetent?'" Ryan paused, then he shook his head.

"Is your Lifeforce intimidated by math or reading?"

He shook his head, smiling softly. "No. It knows I need some help, but I can do it."

With Essence, Ryan had broken through his story of being 'stupid.' Now we could address the issues that would help him move his life in a new direction. We took a few minutes to release his fifth grader—he wanted to go out and play soccer with some friends. When Ryan opened his eyes, he looked composed and relaxed.

Softly, I said, "I'm sorry that school was so hard for you."

He sighed quietly. "Yeah, it really messed with my head."

Now that he had some clarity, it was time to name the elephant in the room. Tenderly, I said, "You know, Ryan, working 'really hard for five days' on a book report tells me that you might have had some learning challenges that impacted your reading skills and probably your math skills as well."

He stared at me quietly. "You think I have a learning disability?"

"That's not my area of expertise, but you can get some testing to find out. If it turns out that you do have some challenges, you can get support to develop these areas. I can give you a referral for a testing center."

Ryan frowned, shaking his head. "I don't know. You can give me the number, but I don't know if I'll call. I don't really see the point."

We spent the rest of the session tending to his discouragement. When he was leaving, I handed him a business card to an assessment center. As he walked out the door, he glanced down at the card, his beautiful bounce gone, his shoulders slumped. Watching him, I imagined the little fifth grader trudging out of the classroom, closing the door on his cognitive wing, never looking back.

Mindsets That Bind Us

When it came to his reading and math difficulties, Ryan had fallen into what Stanford psychology professor Carol Dweck calls a "fixed mindset," the tendency to believe that our present functioning is "fixed," permanent and irreversible. In her book, *Mindset: The New Psychology of Success,* Dr. Dweck differentiates between a fixed mindset and what she calls a "growth mindset," addressing the impact that each can have on our life. People with fixed mindsets tend to believe that we are born with certain innate capacities that make us successful or not, while those with growth mindsets believe that our aptitude in various areas can be cultivated through hard work and proper training.

Those with fixed mindsets often struggle in life. Believing that their conditions are permanent, they often shun new learning, convinced that they will fail if they try new things. When they do fall short in their endeavors, they often blame themselves for being "failures," adding to their shame and pain, cementing their conviction that *nothing will ever change.*

In contrast, those with growth mindsets see their failures as temporary setbacks: "I haven't learned how to do that *yet.*" Inspired, they focus on the excitement of learning itself rather than worrying about the outcome. It is this open, relaxed attitude that allows them to stay engaged with their learning and skill building, thereby increasing the likelihood of successful learning.

In my work with clients, I have found that people have a mixed profile with regards to these mindsets—they have fixed mindsets in some areas, and growth mindsets in others. Ryan was caught in a fixed mindset when it came to math and reading, believing that his academic capacities were permanent and unchangeable. When he considered the demands of the managerial job at Mountains and Rivers, given his current skill level, he felt overwhelmed and disheartened, in other words, "stupid;" a psychological belief that kept him from even considering the possibility of new learning. Listening to Ryan, I was reminded of something Jen said as she talked about her struggling middle schoolers: "A mind can never learn while it's busy beating itself up."

While Ryan may have believed that he could never learn new skills in math and reading, he certainly demonstrated plenty of new learning when it came to outdoor pursuits. As a wilderness guide, he brought a growth mindset to outdoor cognitive learning; he was always willing to learn from his mistakes to increase his skills. Rather than seeing a record of failures when he flipped rafts, ruined camp meals, or made bad choices regarding the weather, Ryan saw these missteps as opportunities to "up his game." If Ryan could bring a growth mindset to his academic challenges, he might see some real improvement that would allow him to "up his game" in math and reading, a shift that would allow him to pursue his dream.

How do we move from a fixed mindset to a growth mindset? It begins with changing our inner story. Dr. Dweck suggests that when we are frustrated in new learning, instead of saying, "I can't..." we should tell ourselves, "Not yet." *I haven't learned how to program yet*. Or *I haven't learned how to surf yet*. "Not Yet" is a mantra that can support us anytime we bump up against cognitive limits as we take on new learning. When we change our inner narrative—whether through reciting positive mantras or releasing our limiting formations—we rewrite our cognitive story. With a growth mindset and ongoing practice, we can all become lifelong learners, able to acquire new knowledge and skills that can bring success to all our domains. If we have

> With a growth mindset and ongoing practice, we can acquire new knowledge and skills that can bring success to all our domains.

developmental challenges, a growth mindset will give us the fortitude we need to do the work it takes to resolve our cognitive issues.

Your Growth and Fixed Mindsets

As you reflect on the Seven Domains—psychological, physical, cognitive, emotional, relational, spiritual, and integrative—in which domains do you have a growth mindset? What narratives do you tell yourself when you hit a "bump" in these areas? In which domains do you hold a fixed mindset? What narratives do you tell yourself as you bump up against challenges in these domains?

Is there a difference in the narratives that you tell yourself in your thriving and struggling domains? As an experiment, apply your growth mindset beliefs (the ones from your thriving domains) to your challenging domains. How does this impact the potential for growth in the domains where you typically struggle?

Developing Our Potential

Ryan may have freed the little boy who believed he was stupid, but he still had work to do if he was going to take up the manager's position at Mountains and Rivers. Since he was clearly struggling with reports and paperwork, I hoped he would take the referral I gave him and get a learning assessment. A learning evaluation would clarify the specific skills he would need to move forward in his life.

When Ryan came in the following week, he had his bounce back and he was sporting a big smile. "Guess what? My boss can't spell! I told him about my math and reading problem, and he told me that if it wasn't for spell check, he'd be out of a job! He also told me that he's always scared people are going to find out about his spelling problem; that they'll think he's stupid." He rolled his eyes playfully. "As if that could happen! Steve's an amazing guide and great businessman. He really knows his stuff."

I smiled warmly. "I'm not surprised to hear about Steve's fears. People often feel ashamed of their cognitive weaknesses, believing it makes them somehow 'not good enough.' I'm glad you talked to him about your struggles; now he can support you as you discuss the management duties."

Ryan leaned back on the couch, looking visibly relieved. "Yeah... He also said that I should take your advice and get tested. He said he wished he'd done it years ago. The spelling thing has bothered him his whole life."

We spent the rest of that session talking about what his new duties as manager would entail. Happily for Ryan, the company's accounting software handled all math calculations, but he still needed some help understanding the spreadsheets and bookkeeping. He would also be drawing up work schedules, running trainings, and handling the employees. "All that's easy, I do that stuff all the time. But there's lots of reports and contracts with the Forest Service, equipment companies, and corporate groups that book the rafting trips. That all feels pretty overwhelming, but Steve's going to meet with me next week to show me the ropes." By the time we finished our session, Ryan was feeling pretty confident that with Steve's support, he could handle the manager's job. As he walked out the door that day, I was pleased to see that he had his bounce in his step.

A week later I got a text message from Ryan cancelling his next two appointments, saying only that he was busy. When we met again, he told me that he had gone to the testing center for the evaluation. Crestfallen, he shared that he had dyslexia and the diagnosis had thrown him into a spiral. "Now what am I supposed to do? I was all ready to take the manager's position, and now I have to deal with this!"

Gently, I said, "You've always been dealing with *this*. But now you know what it is, so you can attend to it."

Looking like a pouty fifth grader, he scowled, "No wonder I was never good at school. The tester said the dyslexia messed with every subject."

"I'm sure it did, but you can turn this around, Ryan. Everyone's built for ongoing learning and development. With the right support, you can address your dyslexia and strengthen your reading and writing skills."

Learning Challenges

If you are struggling with learning, thinking, or organizing, you may benefit from exploring various supports and resources that can help you develop your cognitive skills. You can access supports through adult education centers in your city or town, or access online programs for adult learning. If you think you may have a learning disability, you can access information and support from the Learning Disabilities Association: *www.ldaamerica.org.*

> Just as we can do push-ups, run, and train our body to be stronger and better coordinated, we can become smarter by doing "cognitive push-ups."

Dr. Earl Hunt, a psychologist specializing in human intelligence, likens the process of cognitive development to physical development. Just as we can do push-ups, run, and train our body to be stronger and better coordinated, we can become smarter by doing "cognitive push-ups." With the right tutoring and practice, we can develop our logical reasoning, our critical thinking skills, and build new neural networks that strengthen our mental processing. Anytime we take a class, learn a new skill, apprentice with a mentor, or play brain games, we are strengthening and enlivening our cognitive capacity, building a foundation that can help us live more successfully.

Over the next months, Ryan met regularly with a reading specialist. As his reading skills improved, the contracts and reports at work got easier. Then one day, he eagerly told me that he had checked out a book at the library, one that he had tried to read in high school but never got through it. Although it was challenging, he was working his way through the book.

"It's a great story, I'm really enjoying it!" he said. "If I lose my focus or I can't keep the letters straight, I just take a break, breathe out my stress and rest in my Lifeforce for a minute. When I do that, something releases, and I feel clear and calm again. Then I pick up the book and jump back in. I've started taking "Lifeforce breaks" when I'm at the office; it helps me keep my focus when I get overwhelmed."

I smiled. "That sounds great! Many studies have shown that when people get flustered, it hinders their thinking and processing. When you pause, breathe out your tension, and rest in your Lifeforce, you're calming your mind and body, bringing your 'thinking brain' back online. Reportedly, whenever Albert Einstein got stuck in his work, he would play his violin as he walked around his kitchen. As his mind calmed and settled, new ideas would come to him, allowing him to move ahead with his work."

When we are willing to expand our cognitive abilities, we open ourselves to a richer, more stimulating life. As the manager of Mountains and Rivers, Ryan was enjoying his new capacities and delighting in fresh opportunities to express his potential. Becoming a manager brought Ryan closer to his True Nature—he was a natural leader, and his new role gave him avenues to foster his talents and the maturity that would bring him True Success. These are the gifts of being a lifelong learner. When we make an effort to engage in ongoing development, take up new adventures, and enhance our capacities, we discover new potentials that light up our whole castle.

A Checklist for Success: The Eight Determinants

I hadn't seen Ryan for a few months when he called one day, very excited, asking if we could meet to discuss a new offering he was designing for the company. He was feeling nervous about launching the new program, and he hoped that talking with me might help him calm his nerves.

When he walked in for his appointment, I was immediately struck by his presence. Something in him had settled and matured, and he exuded a confidence I hadn't seen before. We spent a few minutes catching up on his life, then he launched into his project.

"If this idea works, it'll bring in a new revenue stream for the company and expand our presence in the community. I want to offer some avalanche courses and wilderness first-responder trainings. We haven't done a major expansion like this in a long time and Steve is letting me do the whole thing—the planning, the hiring process, everything. I think he's testing me to see if I can really take over the business. He's put a lot of money on the line, so I don't want to blow it." He took a big breath, letting out a stressed sigh. "I know I can release scared formations, but this project has a lot of pieces to it, and I'm trying to stay on top of it."

I smiled encouragingly. "I'm not surprised you're feeling nervous, you're certainly stretching beyond your comfort zone. It sounds like you've tried to be thoughtful in your planning. If it would be helpful, I have a template that we could run it through—a checklist where you can see if you've covered all the bases. It's called the Eight Determinants of Success. Would you be interested in hearing about it?"

Ryan nodded enthusiastically. "Sure! Who doesn't want to guarantee success?! Do you have a pen and paper I could use? I want to take notes."

Handing him a pen and notepad, I said, "Well, there's no *guarantee* for success, but you're more likely to be successful if these eight areas are attended to."

"The first step starts with the *Vision*. If you want to succeed in a venture, you need a clear, specific vision that lays out what you aim to do. For example, there's a big difference between 'We're thinking of offering some trainings,' versus 'We want to offer two Level 1 Avalanche trainings—one in January and February, and two Wilderness First-Responder classes, one in June, and the other one in July.'"

Ryan gave a thumbs-up. "Got it! We have a clear vision."

"Okay, the next determinant has to do with our *Biology*. Do you have the physical ability and cognitive skills needed to pull off your project or goal? For instance, when you wanted to take on the management job at Mountain and Rivers, you certainly had the physical and mental capacity to be a good wilderness leader, but your dyslexia made it hard to navigate the reports and paperwork that came with management. By attending to your learning difficulties, you increased your chances of success as a manager. So, do you have the physical and cognitive skills needed to support these courses?"

Ryan grinned. "Me, personally?! Well, I might teach one course, but I've got some awesome ski instructors and wilderness guides who are totally gifted in these areas."

"Great! Then biology's covered!"

"The next determinant is your *Environment*. Does your present environment support your venture, or does it hold you back? In other words, do you have the resources, people and support to go forward with your idea? When you were going for the management position, you had lots of support from Steve, you came to me for additional support, and you had tutoring from the Learning Center. So do you have the environmental support you need to pull off these courses?"

Ryan reflected a moment, then he nodded thoughtfully. "My friends and the staff are all encouraging me to do it. And Steve's put up the money, paying for the permits and hiring additional staff...and we've got great guides to run the programs... So yeah, I've got lots of support for the program." He stopped to take a couple of notes, then he looked up smiling.

"I'm glad you're feeling supported. Maybe someday you can 'pay it forward' and support someone else as they pursue their dream."

Ryan perked up. "Actually, I'm already doing that. I'm mentoring a couple of guides outside of work and I started a free clinic called 'Little Guides' where we teach kids about wilderness and river safety."

"Wow! Thanks for doing that! That's a great community service, and I'm sure it makes you feel good doing it, which brings us to the next determinant, our *Mind-state*. When we jump into new projects, we need a positive or 'growth' mind-state to sustain us as we navigate the challenges of a new endeavor. If our mind-state is 'off,' we may need to release a formation or unhealthy belief, or if we're 'off' due to a biologic need—let's say, we're 'hangry' or sleep-deprived—we may need to eat some food or get a good night's sleep to get back on track. As you consider your project, are there any mind-states that might sabotage your efforts?"

Ryan grinned sheepishly. "Um...yeah, I definitely have some 'little boys' that are freaking out about disappointing 'Dad.'"

I smiled encouragingly. "Well, you know how to release those formations! And make sure to anchor yourself in your Lifeforce as you go forward on this project. Your Lifeforce has lots of wisdom, it'll make good choices, and it's not worried about Steve's approval." Ryan chuckled and gave me another thumbs-up.

"Now the fifth determinant is *Knowledge and Skills*. Do you have the necessary training and skills to achieve your goal, or do you need more preparation? You clearly have the wilderness and leadership skills to design a good program. But are there any other skills that you might need to develop in order to launch this program?"

Ryan reflected for a moment. "I don't know enough about marketing, but we have a good marketing team. I can talk to them about how best to promote the programs."

"Good. That can help fill the courses and you might learn a thing or two about marketing!"

"The sixth determinant is *Thoughtful Planning and Development*. A good plan lays out the steps we'll take to achieve our goals. If we lose our way, our plan is a 'touchstone' that helps us come back to our goals and vision. But remember, no plan is fixed; sometimes we encounter new conditions or information that requires a shift in our plan. For instance, you may want to offer two avalanche courses, but if you can't find enough instructors, you might have to begin by offering just one course. It's also important to get regular feedback on our projects so it can guide our ongoing planning and development."

Ryan nodded, looking pleased. "We've got a good plan! Steve and I set up a yearlong calendar, along with backup plans, and we have a feedback form for each course."

"Great. That will help you develop a strong program. Okay, the seventh determinant is *Persistent Effort*. As you know from guiding trips, all good projects require consistent, focused work. When we put in the sweat and the hours, we're more likely to get the results we want.

"And finally, the last determinant is *Life Happens*. No matter how well we plan and prepare, Life has the final word. Sometimes Life undoes our plans; you may want to do a cliff ascent, and it rains. Other times, Life brings opportunities. If Steve hadn't approached you about the manager's position, you may never have addressed your learning difficulties. In that instance, Life brought you a gift."

Ryan smiled. "I never thought about it that way! You're right, I probably wouldn't have taken on the math and reading if Steve hadn't offered me the position. It sure didn't feel like a gift back then! But I'm glad I went through it; I feel like I'm living a new life—a great life! I'm actually trying to get Steve to go to the Learning Center. I think he'd be a lot happier if he dealt with his spelling problem."

After reviewing the Eight Determinants, Ryan was feeling a lot more optimistic about his new project, and I was delighting in how this playful wilderness guide had become an inspiring leader both at Mountains and Rivers and within the community. By attending to his undeveloped faculties, Ryan had come to exemplify the vision of True Success: *Living our True Nature as best we can, right here in this moment and helping others to do the same.*

A year later, I ran into Ryan at an outdoor gear swap. He told me that the new programs had taken off; they were bringing in new revenue and he had requests for new trainings—a development that made him very happy. He also told me that he had begun negotiations with Steve to buy the business from him.

"I never thought I'd own a business! Who knew that the Cognitive Domain would make me so successful!"

I laughed. "Actually, the Cognitive Domain has always made you successful; you just brought your math and reading up to speed, which allowed you to move into bigger roles—ones where your True Nature really shines. I'm sure you'll take Mountains and Rivers in great directions."

Ryan beamed. "Thanks for the vote of confidence! I am excited about it! It's a dream come true!"

Being a lifelong learner is one of the superpowers of True Success. As we aim for a more successful life, learning is the doorway to realizing our dreams, passions, and potential. We might go back to school, apprentice with a mentor, study YouTube videos, or take an online class. When we release our limiting, self-defeating stories and take up a growth mindset, we can improve our academic skills, our physical skills, our emotional skills, our relational skills, and our spiritual faculties, opening ourselves to a more enlivened, fascinating life. With the support of our Cognitive Domain, we can grow and evolve at any time in our life, sharpening the "brains behind the wheel" that steer us in the direction of a vibrant, fulfilling future.

> As we aim for a more successful life, learning is the doorway to realizing our dreams, passions, and potential.

The Eight Determinants of Success

Below are eight factors that shape the success of any goal or project. Meeting these criteria will increase the likelihood of success in any arena.

Vision: Do you have a clear vision of your goal or project? Be specific and name exactly what you intend to do.

Biology: Do you have the physical capacity to do your project? If not, what special accommodations do you need (physical aids, training, medication, or assistance), to achieve your goal?

Environment: Do you have the resources, the people, and the support to go forward in a sustained way? If not, where can you get these supports?

Mind-state: Are you supporting your vision with a growth mindset, along with adequate rest, healthy food, necessary medications, releasing formations, and connecting with Essence?

Knowledge and Skills: Do you have the training needed to succeed in your endeavor? If not, where can you get the necessary training?

Thoughtful Planning and Development: Do you have a clear plan on how you will meet your goals? Do you have a "Plan B should conditions change?"

Persistent Effort: Are you prepared to put in consistent, focused effort? Success requires perseverance.

Life Happens: Is Life supporting this venture? If not, stop and take a pause. It may not be the right time to launch your project, you may have to rethink what you are doing, or there may be a different path calling to you.

The Emotional Domain
The Freedom to Feel Everything

In a rich and fulfilling life, emotions are the spice that bring vibrancy and color to our days. Love, joy, hate, fear, sadness, and grief infuse our life with energy and vitality, making us feel truly *alive*. Love and happiness bring excitement and bliss, while grief, sadness, and fear reveal just how deeply we cherish our loved ones and life itself. It is emotions that make falling in love exciting, sunsets compelling, home cooking taste amazing, and holding a child, a blessing beyond words.

What exactly are emotions? Beyond the simple fact that they are feelings (I use *feelings* and *emotions* interchangeably), emotions are mental states entwined with physical sensations that express the psychological meanings we are attributing to our experience at any given moment. The word "emotion" comes from the Old French word *emouvoir*, meaning "to stir up," and emotions certainly stir us up, physically and mentally. We may yell with excitement, jumping up and down as our team scores a goal. We may cringe with fear and nausea as we peer over the edge of a high bridge. We might feel a heavy weight overtake us as we collapse in sadness upon hearing of a friend's death. Or we may sigh with delight as we sink into our partner's hug or snuggle with our pet. With emotions, the mind and body are always linked in partnership, expressing our human experience.

The mind/body experience of emotions arises through an ebb and flow of neurochemicals surging through our body. When we are excited or scared, *adrenaline* rushes through our bloodstream causing an increase in energy, sweating, and a faster heartbeat. When we are sad, *decreases in serotonin* makes us feel heavy and numb. When we are relaxed in comfort or pleasure, *dopamine* and *oxytocin* flow, making us happy, warm, and comfy.

The flow and intensity of these neurochemicals creates the spectrum of our emotions. When these biochemicals are diminished, our emotions are subtle and barely perceptible. When they are surging and abundant, our emotions are stormy and overwhelming. For example, with sadness, we can go from mild disappointment to sorrow, grief, melancholy, all the way to depression. With anger, the range can run from frustrated to irate, upset, mad, or explosive with rage. With fear, we may feel uneasy, worried, anxious, panicked, or terrified. And with joy, we may feel happy, delighted, jubilant, delirious, or maniacally exuberant. When we experience a healthy range of emotions, life feels rich, stimulating, and meaningful, but if our emotions become intolerable, life can feel unbearable.

When our emotions are out of balance, we can be pulled into a whirlwind of feelings and sensations. In what is known as *hyper-arousal*, emotions may reveal themselves as panic, anxiety, rage, or mania. In *hypo-arousal*, emotions and sensations express as heaviness, confusion, and lethargy; we may feel inconsolably numb, hopeless, empty, or depressed. When we are caught up in these extreme states, we don't feel in control of our feelings: We can't stop crying or grieving. We are always depressed. We keep having panic attacks. Or we are stuck in rage, unable to pull ourselves out of it. Other times, we may swing rapidly between different emotions; one minute we feel calm, and the next, we are flooded with fear, sadness, despondency, or anxiety. When we are consumed by emotional turmoil, it's hard to attend to our daily tasks—we may emotionally "lose it" to the point where we collapse or explode—derailing our work, our relationships, or generally making a mess of our life. When we are experiencing emotional dysregulation, it's hard to create a successful life.

If we find ourselves out of emotional balance, we need to bring ourselves back onto solid ground, otherwise, we may lose the gains we have worked so hard to achieve. Sometimes, we may need the support of a psychotherapist, or use medications to soothe the neurochemicals that are fueling our emotional upheaval. Other times, we may engage in biofeedback, nutritional consultations, hypnosis, or healing ceremonies. And in some cases, we might engage in alternative therapies such as psychedelic therapies, which have been shown to alleviate depression and panic in those suffering from terminal illnesses and PTSD. In addition to these therapies, we may need to make significant life changes to shift out of our emotional distress: We may need to leave a stressful job, stop abusing drugs or alcohol, or get out of an abusive situation so we can bring ourselves back into emotional balance. As is often the case, when we get our life in balance, our emotions get in balance.

Neurochemicals may be the agent of our emotions, but it is our inner narratives that most often fire up our neurochemicals. If your friend doesn't reach out to you on your birthday and you believe it's because *they are mad at you*, you may suddenly feel anxious. But if you believe their silence means that *they are overwhelmed* in their life, you are more likely to feel warmth and compassion for them, secure in the belief that you are still lovingly connected. For this reason, we can say that *meanings make emotions*. The meanings we attribute to events determine the emotions we will feel—negative meanings bring negative emotions; positive meanings bring positive emotions.

> The meanings we attribute to events determines the emotions we will feel.

The meanings we give to particular events arise out of our own past conditioning, and this is particularly true of our emotional conditioning. If we watched our parents happily relax into hugs with others, saying, "I love you!" and heard them speak about how "nice" hugs were, we likely learned to feel joyous and relaxed when offered a hug. But if our parents froze anytime someone hugged them, or we heard them say that hugs were "sappy" or "unnecessary," there's a good chance that we came to feel uneasy and awkward about showing our love with a hug. Similarly, if we saw our parents cry when they were touched by beauty or tenderness, we carry an inner permission to cry during tender moments. But if they were stoic, even in the face of great pain, we learned to suppress our feelings.

Given our emotional upbringing, there may be times when we consciously set out to develop emotional responses in direct opposition to the way we were raised. For instance, if your mother was exceptionally teary and depressed all the time, you may consciously strive to never cry, always keeping yourself emotionally positive and optimistic. If your father was angry and mean, you may work hard to be kind and contain your anger.

As you reflect on your emotional upbringing, are there any emotions that you deliberately avoid in reaction to your past? If so, what would it *mean* to express those emotions? Asking this question may uncover the psychological meanings and stories that are driving your emotional expression.

Our emotional expression is also influenced by social conventions. All humans experience love, joy, fear, shame, disgust, and sadness, but how we express these emotions is greatly shaped by our culture. All societies have "rules" that govern emotional expression given our gender, age, class, and status. For example, in the United States, anger is more readily tolerated from men but often regarded as "bitchy" or "unlady-like" when expressed by women. Likewise, children are permitted to be exuberant, silly, and spontaneous in their emotions, while adults are encouraged to be more reserved. Religions also decree which emotions are considered acceptable or unacceptable—love and compassion are considered "saintly" and "virtuous," while powerful desires and feelings such as hatred and jealousy are labeled as "bad" or "sinful."

As you reflect on your upbringing, which feelings were encouraged and supported? *Love... joy... grief... anger?* Which feelings were shunned or frowned upon? *Love... joy... grief... anger?* Were you ever punished for expressing emotions? If so, which ones? In truth, many of us grew up with confusing messages about emotions. For instance, it may have been okay to show anger toward our siblings, but we were told to "hold our tongue" with parents and adults out of respect for elders. We may have grown up watching television ads that promoted fun, sexy play, but when we expressed ourselves in fun, sexy ways, we were told that we were being "ridiculous" or "slutty." And some of us were teased or shamed every time we cried or showed our fear. As you reflect on your emotional life, do you feel permission to express your full emotional aliveness? If not, are there any "rules" you would like to let go of?

Given the complexity and messiness of emotions, some of us may have decided that the world would be better off without emotions—everything would be better if we could just be rational and analytical. But as anyone who has watched *Star Trek* knows, even logical Spock and Data, who typically shunned emotions, realized that emotions serve a vital function in our intelligence for they play a key role in informing and guiding our decisions. It is our emotions that alert us when something is good for us, and when something is amiss. If we feel unhappy about our weight or health, our emotional discomfort can spur us on to eat well and exercise. In the same manner, it is our joy in having a healthier body that inspires us to continue our healthy eating and exercise. In a similar way, the pride and satisfaction we feel in having great technological skills can inspire us to expand our computer science knowledge. But if we misuse our abilities, let's say...to build a program to swindle people out of their money, it is our fear and guilt that gets us to reconsider our actions and dismantle the database. The moment-to-moment emotional "feedback" we receive about our choices and actions helps us choose a path to a more successful life.

Emotions also play a significant role in domain development. In the domains where we are most successful, we tend to experience more joy and have greater emotional resilience. For example, if you excel in the Physical Domain, you likely enjoy physical pursuits and readily bounce back anytime you encounter difficulties or setbacks while playing sports, climbing a mountain, or physically training. If you excel in the Cognitive Domain, you may love programming, organizing, or learning about new things, and you can quickly re-center yourself when you encounter frustrations in your projects.

Reflecting on your Seven Domains, where do you experience the most emotional stability and freedom? Which domains bring the most frustration and emotional collapse? As you learn to release the negative formations in your challenging domains, you will discover much more freedom and joy in these arenas, which will help you develop your potential.

True Success in the Emotional Domain brings greater freedom and aliveness to all areas of our life. How do we cultivate this freedom and resilience? We do this by developing our *emotional intelligence*. With emotional intelligence, we can identify and work with our own and others' emotions in ways that promote healthy, successful outcomes. With emotional intelligence:

- We understand how emotions arise and know how to work with them.
- We are comfortable with the full spectrum of emotions—mild to wild.
- We can calm our emotions when they become overwhelming.
- We engage in practices that support healthy emotional development.
- We express our feelings in ways that serve us and the world, not harm it.

With emotional intelligence, we have the skills to navigate life with grace and steadiness, and we are able to experience the full spectrum of our feelings in ways that are healthy and rewarding. Emotional intelligence also brings *emotional resilience*—the ability to calm ourselves and "bounce back" from stress to reclaim mental stability, clear thinking, and positive emotions—often in the present moment. With emotional resilience, we can ride the ups and downs of life without getting caught up in reactivity and negative emotions: we can stay calm when our coworkers get on our nerves; we can meet our child's tantrums with clarity and kindness; and we can remain loving and connected during stressful family gatherings. On Life's emotional rollercoaster, we can learn to flow with joy, sorrow, grief, love, anger, and passion and not get unseated. When we embrace our feelings and use them to guide us, we can't help but create a truly successful life.

Discovering Your Emotional Resilience

In which areas of your life are you emotionally resilient, in other words, in what situations do you quickly "bounce back" from fear, sadness, grief, or anger? What beliefs about yourself and your experience allow you to rebound from these negative emotional experiences? Perhaps you tell yourself, "This is only temporary," or "I can get through this." Maybe you believe that these difficulties will strengthen you to be a better person. It is these kinds of positive beliefs and meanings (expressions of a growth mindset), that hold the key to your emotional resilience.

Caught in Negative Emotions

On a warm spring day, I returned from a lunch hour walk to prepare for my next appointment—a client who was coming in for their first session. Opening the door to my waiting room, I was surprised to see a gentle looking man leaning against the large picture window, staring down at the street below. He looked as if he was carrying a great weight on his shoulders, so I offered him a warm hello. He turned, said, "Hi" and walked past me into the office. I followed him in and closed the door softly, gesturing to him to take a seat.

"I'm glad to meet you, Carlos. What brings you here?" On his intake form, he had written that he was having difficulty at work.

"I hate my life," he said, sounding tired and defeated. "I just turned forty and I would say that I'm having a mid-life crisis, but I haven't even had a life yet. I haven't done anything interesting, exciting, or worth mentioning. I just take care of other people."

"Are you a caretaker?"

"No. I work as a travel agent booking people's trips, and I help out my parents."

"So, you take care of others... What do you like to do in your free time?"

He shrugged. "When I get home at night, I watch travel shows and play video games."

"Do you travel much yourself?"

"No, but I would *love* to. There are so many places I would visit, Europe... I'd like to see the castles, the museums, the history, the Acropolis... I'd see it all. But I'm never going to get there."

Carlos told me that he had spent his childhood devouring books on medieval knights, castles, and the great kingdoms of Europe. He loved King Arthur, medieval music, jousting and chivalry and he had taken this passion straight into his job at the travel agency. He had started out at the agency as the director's assistant, but with his vast knowledge of Europe, he was quickly promoted to agent. As their European travel specialist, Carlos couldn't believe that he was getting *paid* to research medieval castles and history.

"It sounds like you found the perfect work," I said, warmly.

"I love my job, or at least I used to... I thought if I worked for a travel agency, I would travel all over. But I've been there ten years, and I still haven't gone anywhere."

"So, what's stopping you?"

Carlos sighed heavily. "I have responsibilities—my parents, my apartment, my work, my cat..."

"Your cat?"

He cracked a small smile. "Mr. Gato. He's very possessive."

"So, you'd like to travel, but your responsibilities are holding you back."

He sighed sullenly. "Yeah, it's just not in the cards."

I took some time to gather additional information, and as we spoke, I noticed that Carlos framed everything in heavy, negative terms—everything in his life was described as a burden, a chore, or oppressive. It was clear that Carlos was trapped in a cycle of depressive emotions, but before we could attend to his deeper issues, we would need to loosen the grip of the heaviness he was caught in.

"Carlos, since you're feeling pretty despondent, would you be open to doing an exercise that might shift your mood?"

He nodded sullenly. "If you think it will help."

I smiled kindly. "I do think it will help! Why don't you rest against the couch and close your eyes, or if you prefer, you can look softly at the floor, not looking at anything in particular, that way you won't get visually distracted and go into lots of thinking." Carlos closed his eyes and leaned back against the cushions.

"Now, you said that you don't have much going on in your life except for work, and this is making you feel disheartened. As an antidote to these feelings, I'd like you to name a few things that you're grateful for—things that you're glad you have in your life—it can be anything that comes to mind."

Carlos grimaced. "I don't know…"

Kindly, I said, "Humor me, for a moment."

He gave a tiny smile. "Okay, um… I like my job. I'm glad I have Mr. Gato…" He was silent a moment. "I like playing medieval video games and the people I play with…" He exhaled, relaxing a bit. "I'm glad it's nice outside today because I walked here… I like working with Jerry; he's a guy at work, he's funny. I like Big City burritos, they're the best. And I'm glad that I'm healthy." He went on for another minute or two, and as he did, his voice began to lighten, and he settled more deeply into the couch. When he opened his eyes, he looked more relaxed.

> When
> we lighten our
> mind, we lighten our
> emotions. When our
> inner narrative shifts,
> our feelings follow.

"So how are you feeling, having named some things that are good in your life?"

He nodded. "It feels good."

"I'm glad that was helpful. When we are feeling stuck in negative feelings, it can feel a bit consuming. But if we shift the content of our mind—by naming our gratitudes or changing the stories that we're focusing on—we can actually shift our emotions; when we lighten our mind, we lighten our emotions. When our inner narrative shifts, our feelings follow."

Gratitude Practice

At any point in your day, give yourself a moment to take some deep, clearing breaths. As you settle, ask yourself what you are grateful for right now in your life—it may be people, events, your work, your pets, or the tree outside your house. As you acknowledge and name what you are grateful for, notice how this gratitude influences your mind, body, and heart. You may notice that your shoulders soften, your breath relaxes, or your mind feels calmer. You may even feel a sense of joy. When our inner narrative shifts, our feelings follow. As you note these positive feelings, breathe the joy and ease throughout your body; this will help you bring the peace and ease with you into your day.

Emotions mirror our thoughts. If we focus on hopeless thoughts, we feel hopeless. Scary thoughts stir up fear. And soothing thoughts help us feel relaxed. By offering Carlos a Gratitude Practice, I invited him to call up uplifting supports that nourish him, shifting his inner focus from pain and sorrow to being held and nurtured. It was this shift in perspective that allowed him to feel "good." The positive emotions that come with Gratitude Practice can give us a mini vacation from our stress. Gratitude can help us get back on solid ground, fostering emotional resilience.

Beyond Gratitude Practice, there are other ways to shift our mind away from negative thoughts. We can offer ourselves Loving Kindness, repeat positive affirmations, or recite healing mantras that bathe our mind with peace, positivity, and joy. Meditation and yoga also bring calm and equanimity to our heart. And if we treat ourselves to a massage or listen to soothing music, it can help us relax, releasing mind-states of hopelessness, anxiety, or depression. Physical exercise can also bring positive emotions—as we work out, the release of endorphins counters the taxing neurochemicals that come with stress. Anytime we engage in healthy, comforting practices, we give rise to uplifting emotions that move our life in a positive direction.

In that first session, I wanted to show Carlos that it was possible to step out of his misery and to open to the prospect of living differently. Soon, I would introduce him to the peace and ease of Essence, a refuge that would liberate him from his depressing feelings. As he got up to leave that day, I encouraged him to use Gratitude Practice as a way to stay in touch with more positive emotions.

"As you walk back to work, you might name some gratitudes along the way," I suggested. "You might enjoy seeing the sun shining through the trees, hearing the sounds of birds singing, or taking in the scents of spring. As you do this, note how these small, positive things can brighten your mood and lighten your mind and heart. When you come back next time, I'll show you a practice that can help you feel happier and give you some emotional resilience."

Carlos nodded appreciatively. "Thanks. I'll try the gratitudes on my way back to work. I could use a break from feeling terrible."

Negative Emotions: Friend or Foe?

Carlos had found his dream job, but he wasn't living a truly successful life. His belief that caring for others meant *he could never travel* had left him feeling boxed in and hopeless. In the same way that our psychological beliefs impact our body and our cognitive processing, they also color our emotional experience. Anytime we believe that we must forsake our deep passions, it's easy to become depressed, angry, jealous, forlorn, or numb. When we are not living authentically, expressing our True Nature, our daily pursuits can feel empty and unsatisfying. We may have a prestigious job with plenty of money, but if our heart is not in the work, our week can feel like an abyss of dread and drudgery. If we are with the wrong partner, we can go out for expensive dinners and take fancy vacations with them, but it all feels dull and unsatisfying. This is not to say that life should be without challenges; obstacles are part of everyday life. But if we are ignoring the calling of our heart, our life may hold little joy and satisfaction, for something is always missing.

The most common form of despair is not being who you are.
—*Soren Kierkegaard*

Difficult emotions always point to a condition that wants attention—a wound not healed, a dream unrealized, a truth not told— hounding us until we turn and listen to what is beckoning.

While negative emotions may feel awful, they hold a silver lining. Our heart will make us miserable if we refuse to listen to the "still small voice" that calls us to a truly successful life. It is our negative emotions that compel us to grow beyond our barriers and do the inner work needed so we can fulfill our dreams and ambitions. Difficult emotions always point to a condition that wants attention—a wound not healed, a dream unrealized, a truth not told— hounding us until we turn and listen to what is beckoning.

A few weeks into our work, Carlos arrived for his appointment looking despondent and miserable. "I'm sick of booking other people's trips. I was working on a client's trip this morning, and all I kept thinking was, *Why do they get to go the Acropolis? They won't even appreciate it!* I'm so jealous of other people! Why do they get to do what they want, while I'm stuck here? I'm starting to hate my job, and I don't want to hate my job, it's the best thing I've got going in my life. Maybe I should get some pills. Then I could just calm down and get back to doing my job without feeling horrible."

I smiled sympathetically. "I'm not surprised that you're feeling jealous and angry, Carlos, but I don't think you're at a point where you need medication. I think you're feeling terrible because you're neglecting your heart's desires and you're trying to deny your feelings."

"Jealousy isn't a problem, Carlos. It's an alarm clock, waking you up to the fact that something is "off" in your life. The same thing is at play anytime we feel anger, craving, guilt, or hatred. Jealousy is telling you that the life you're living right now, feels too small. You're living in the broom closet of your castle, and you're not getting out to explore the other wings. Why don't we start working on the things that are holding you back, so you can step out of that broom closet and start living your own fulfilling life."

I invited Carlos to get comfortable and close his eyes. When he was mindfully settled, I broached his dreaded issue. "So, I'd like you to consider taking a trip to Europe. I know this may not be easy..." Carlos shook his head with annoyance and opened his eyes.

"I CAN'T go to Europe! Why don't you understand that?! I have to take care of my parents—they're immigrants! They don't speak English well, they have a hard time negotiating ANYTHING, and now that they're older..." he wavered.

"They rely on you more?"

Carlos huffed in exasperation. "Yeah!"

"So, if you follow your dreams..."

"Then I'm not a 'good' son!" He leaned back and ran his fingers through his hair, sighing in frustration.

"What are you noticing right now?"

"That my life sucks and it's never going to change! I feel pissed off and pinned in and I'm sick of this! I'm their only kid, and it's always been this way!"

"What do you mean, 'It's always been this way?'"

With my question, he deflated, sinking into heaviness. "When I was seventeen, I saved a few thousand dollars mowing lawns and doing odd jobs. I was planning on spending the summer in Europe for my eighteenth birthday. I wanted to see all the King Arthur stuff, the castles...*everything*. I was so excited. I was going to be traveling on my own, seeing the places I love... But when my dad found out, he exploded. 'Who's going to cut the grass and do the yard work? What if your mother gets sick? Who's going to translate for us at the hospital, did you ever think of that?!! What kind of son goes off and leaves his parents?! A selfish one! That's what you are!' My mom just sat there nodding silently, agreeing with him. He made me feel like I was the worst son in the world!"

"And you're still living out that story."

He huffed with all the defiance of a seventeen-year-old. "Yeah! And it's never going to change! So stop talking to me about traveling!"

When we deny our own passions and potential, it's easy to feel jealous, frustrated, "fed up," or angry. Our anger and frustration may embolden us to not feel like a victim, but it rarely moves us in the direction we want to go. Most often, our anger and frustration simply blow off steam, or we direct our anger onto others to no avail—just as when Carlos got mad at his clients for going to Greece, or he told me, "Stop talking about traveling!" If Carlos wanted to live a happy, fulfilling life, he needed to get beyond his anger and deepen into the formations that were keeping him locked in a confined life.

Meeting the Gatekeeper

In my work with clients, I often find that before we can access the tender, pained formations that hold us back, we must first contend with fierce, emotional formations, which I call *gatekeepers*. Gatekeepers are like those fierce giant statues that stand guard outside the entrances of ancient sacred temples in the East. Ferocious and imposing, they bare their sharp teeth and claws, warding off anything that may be threatening. Carlos's anger and frustration were serving as gatekeepers, keeping both of us from accessing the tender pain that lay at the heart of his problem—the belief that in order to be a good son, he had to forgo his dreams.

Like other formations, most gatekeepers form in childhood as a response to our suffering. If we weren't allowed to experience vulnerable feelings, or we were overwhelmed by painful emotions, we developed protective formations that rose to our defense, standing guard outside our tender heart. Imagine for a moment, a young child being called "Shorty." The child's feelings would be understandably hurt, leaving them feeling sad and dejected. If that taunting happens just once and the child receives support and understanding, the emotional pain releases and a formation does not form. But if the name-calling continues for years, the child will try to circumvent the pain: They may spend their days avoiding their peers, staying in at recess, or receding into the background at social gatherings, hoping not to be noticed and picked on, until one day when they are older, someone calls out, "Hey, Shorty!" and they've had enough! "Oh yeah?! Well, I'm gonna keep growing, but 'stupid' is forever! And you're stupid!" The gatekeeper has emerged, and it doesn't look anything like a sad, pained child.

> Anytime anger, overreaction, irritation, condescension, hysterics, rage, or collapse are "stirring up" the room, we are in the presence of a gatekeeper.

Gatekeepers often express the very opposite of what we are feeling at a deeper level. Angry gatekeepers may cover over sadness. Collapsed and teary gatekeepers can conceal anger and frustration. Blustery and arrogant gatekeepers can camouflage fear and shame. In many ways, gatekeepers work as a smoke screen, keeping the tender one well-hidden from view. Anytime anger, overreaction, irritation, condescension, hysterics, rage, or collapse are "stirring up" the room, we are in the presence of a gatekeeper. If we keep in mind that these responses are protective in nature, it can help us not personalize the attack and give us a compassionate perspective. Gatekeepers may look indomitable, but with the right attention, they often calm down and step aside.

When we encounter a gatekeeper in others, taking a moment to ground ourselves in Essence can bring a calming stability that invites deeper, more vulnerable emotions. For example, if you ask your brother if he's coming for the holidays and he blows up at you, you've met a gatekeeper. Instead of reacting with anger yourself, you can relax into Essence and ask yourself, "What's really going on with him?" Perhaps, you'll see fear in his eyes. Seeing this, you can respond with compassion. Your response may even soften his defenses—his gatekeeper might dissolve, and he may confide to you that he doesn't have the money to buy tickets for everyone in his family to travel during the holidays.

The same holds true when encountering our own gatekeepers. If we see that we are being overreactive, taking a moment to step back into our Essence can put us in touch with the part of ourselves that is calm and centered, giving us the inner stability to deepen down into our own pain and fear. Gatekeepers may be fierce, but they love it when a calm "grown-up" is in the room. In the presence of a safe, mature adult, they often relax and step aside, giving full access to the tender one.

> A life built around self-protection is a life not fully lived.

While it is important to honor and respect gatekeepers for their work in keeping us safe, we don't want them to rule our life. A life built around self-protection is a life not fully lived. If we believe that our gatekeepers and other formations are who we really are, we are only living part of our full potential, especially when it comes to our emotional life. If Carlos could let go his gatekeeper, he could access and release the tender one who was confining him to an unfulfilled destiny. Doing so would allow him to change his life's trajectory to create a more gratifying life.

True Emotional Resilience

I didn't believe Carlos' gatekeeper when it shouted at me that the best course of action was to "stop talking about traveling." That would only leave Carlos feeling despondent. So, I gently stepped in to shift the direction of the conversation.

"This anger you're feeling is pretty strong." I looked kindly at him, not wanting to deny his gatekeeper, but knowing it would have to step aside for Carlos to move ahead. He glared at me silently, so I continued. "If this anger could talk to your parents, what would it want to say to them?"

He sneered. "What would it say? It would say, 'Take care of your own stuff and leave me alone!' But I'm not going to say that to them."

"And why wouldn't you?" I asked gently.

Carlos looked around the room as if he was looking for the answer. Huffing in exasperation, he grumbled, "Because it's mean. Because I don't want to hurt them. Because..." his face fell. Looking like a little boy, he said, "Because my dad would blow up if I did." The angry teen had given way to a sad, scared boy.

Softly, I said, "I imagine this fear of your dad is what's *really* holding you back. Would it be okay to work with this?"

Carlos nodded sullenly. "Sure. But it won't change anything. My dad's pretty bullheaded."

I invited him to close his eyes. "Let's go back to that seventeen-year-old again." Carlos closed his eyes and sighed heavily. "What feelings come up as your dad is yelling at you?"

"I'm mad at him."

"Are there any other feelings?"

"I'm scared of him, if that's what you mean."

"Go ahead and let yourself feel that fear. What's it like?"

"I don't like it. I feel shaky. I've always been scared of him, he's a big guy."

"That makes sense. Dads can be really intimidating. So as you notice this fear, can you take a step back and feel the quiet of Essence in the background?" He was quiet for a moment, then nodded.

"Let yourself breathe into that Essence, resting in its refuge." I gave him a moment to settle. "Now, bring Essence into that memory with your dad. Essence is standing there, and your dad's yelling at you... Does Essence feel sad or scared?" Carlos paused, then shook his head, no.

"Is Essence feeling 'pinned in' by your parents' needs?"

"No. It's calm...almost neutral."

"And importantly, is Essence *selfish*?"

"Selfish?"

"Yes. Your father said that you were a selfish person. As you feel into the presence of Essence, is it selfish? Is your inner nature selfish?"

Carlos paused, then a soft smile lit his face. "No, it's not selfish. It's relaxed and peaceful. It doesn't want to hurt my parents; it cares about them."

I invited him to anchor this new insight. "Take a moment to savor this, *to know for yourself* that you are not a selfish person; you are kind and caring."

He let out a long sigh. "That's a relief. I guess I always thought I was selfish."

"You are a good, caring person, Carlos. You can trust your inherent goodness." I gave him a moment to feel the poignancy of sensing his True Nature.

"When we are connected to our inherent goodness, Carlos—our True Nature—we have the foundation we need to live authentically. Seeing the purity of our heart and our intentions, allows us to trust the guidance of our own heart, our North Star, which holds the desires and values that make us feel alive and 'complete.' As you said earlier, you don't want to hurt your parents. You're simply called to desires that enliven your heart."

"So as you're standing there in Essence…your father is angry, yelling that you need to take care of them, telling you that you're selfish if you don't… What does Essence see? What's really going on with him?"

Carlos was silent for a moment. When he spoke, his voice was clear and strong. "He's raging, but he's actually afraid. He's scared that I'm going to leave and never come back, like they did. They left their families in Mexico to move here, and they don't have any family around them. He's scared of losing me; he thinks that they can't get along without me."

"And how does Essence feel towards him, seeing all this?"

Quietly he said, "I feel compassion for him…and I can see that they're strong and resourceful. They're fine."

"And how does Essence feel about you traveling?"

Carlos reflected a moment, then smiled. "I can travel. It's not selfish, it's self-preserving. They'll be okay."

We spent the next few minutes releasing his seventeen-year-old. Not surprisingly, he wanted to go explore castles. As Carlos rested in Essence with his eyes closed, I asked him to describe his present experience, naming two qualities that were present now.

With a soft grin, he said, "I feel excited, like I can do this…and that makes me happy."

"That's great! So, take a moment to breathe this excitement and happiness throughout your body so you can carry it with you when you leave."

"For Europe?"

I laughed. "I meant when you leave the office today. But yes, even better, when you leave for Europe."

When Carlos opened his eyes, he looked pleased and happy.

"So, what was it like being in Essence as you faced your father's anger?"

He nodded brightly. "It was good! In Essence, I didn't feel any anxiety and I didn't need his approval. I knew I was a good person and I felt calm while he was freaking out. It was almost like I was the parent."

I nodded. "Essence does have qualities of a strong, competent adult. Grounded in its own integrity, it doesn't need acceptance from others. It rests in the wisdom it gleans from seeing conditions clearly. Do you remember how I told you that 'meanings make emotions?'" He nodded. "As a teen, your father's anger and shaming meant to you that you were a 'bad son.' But in Essence, you saw that his anger was actually a shield— what I call a gatekeeper—covering over his fear about losing his family or not being able to get by given his struggles with English. In Essence, you saw his anger as a reflection of his suffering and that meaning awakened compassion in you. When we are in Essence, we can see others' True Nature *and* their suffering, and with this clarity, Essence makes different meanings, so its 'emotions' are balanced and loving."

> When we are grounded in the refuge of our Essence, we have true emotional resilience.

When we are resting in the calm of Essence, we don't get swept up in negative emotions. We may still feel the stressful emotions of our formations, but we aren't entangled with the experience, getting yanked this way and that. If something upsetting happens, we can feel pain and discomfort, but with Essence we also feel the part of us that is bigger than the afflictive emotions, and this perspective allows us to express our hurt and anger in ways that promote well-being for everyone involved. In scary moments, we may feel fear, but instead of being overwhelmed by it, with Essence we have the clear insight and strength to meet what we're facing. And when others are mean or cruel to us, we may feel a wave of anxiety or shame, but Essence allows us to feel calm and even compassionate toward the aggressors, allowing us to deal with their gatekeepers in effective ways. When we are grounded in the refuge of our Essence, we have true emotional resilience. No matter what is happening, we have a refuge that feels safe, allowing us to respond with wisdom and kindness, living our life in a way that's aligned with our values, morals, and passions.

The Freedom to Follow Our Dreams

At our next appointment, Carlos came in with a to-do list of preparations for his European trip. "I'll need your help on how to talk to my parents; that's going to be hard. But I thought of some ideas that might help them relax about my traveling. I talked to my friend Luis and he's willing to check in on them while I'm gone, and he can translate for them if they need it. He's already been over for a few dinners with my parents, so they're comfortable with him. And I'll leave Mr. Gato with them. They like cats—and that way, they'll know I'm coming back. I would never abandon Mr. Gato."

"So, Mr. Gato's their return voucher?"

He grinned. "Yeah, he's travel insurance."

Carlos spent the next few months building a new relationship with his parents, one where he felt more like an equal. As he navigated this new territory, we continued to release the formations that arose with each step of the process. Sometimes he felt like a little boy, afraid of being in trouble with his parents. Other times he felt frustrated that they didn't immediately accept his ideas. But with each release, Carlos was becoming stronger and finding his voice: He was having powerful conversations with his parents and renegotiating what it meant to be a "good son." He was also clear with them that he would now be traveling, fulfilling his lifelong passion and following his dreams, just as they had done when they moved to the States. As Carlos opened to the joy and satisfaction of planning his own upcoming trip, he also fell in love with his work again.

Six months after our first session, Carlos went on his first European tour. When he returned, he was bubbling with excitement as he told me all about his adventures. Listening to him, I smiled. "Living the life you love, looks good on you!"

He laughed heartily. "Yeah, I am feeling pretty happy these days! And I think my parents are happier too. They've adopted Mr. Gato as their grandchild, and Luis is now their second son. He's invited to all the Sunday dinners."

We sat quietly for a few moments, savoring Carlos's achievements. When he spoke again, he was full of warmth and appreciation. "Thank you for your help. I feel like I'm finally living *my* life."

I smiled warmly. "You've done a lot of work to realize your dreams, Carlos! You have good practices to keep you clear and centered… You've shifted the dynamics with your parents… I don't think you'll be having a mid-life crisis now; you're actually having a mid-life awakening."

His eyes widened. "I am having a mid-life awakening! And I do have good practices to keep me going. You know how I like making itineraries? Well, I made up my own 10-10-10 itinerary. I have this mindfulness app on my phone, where I set the bell to ring every ten minutes for a half hour. For the first ten minutes, I focus on breathing out any stress, anxiety or sadness I'm feeling that day. Then for the next ten minutes, I release any formations that are around: There might be a little boy who's scared because my boss flipped out at work…or an angry teenager who's mad at Mr. Gato for digging up my plants… After I do the releases, I spend the last ten minutes resting in Essence, feeling peaceful and content. I started doing it while I was in Europe, and it helped me stay calm, even on days when I had travel issues."

"Carlos, that's awesome! Do you mind if I share this with others?"

He smiled. "Go ahead! You can call it, 'The Carlos Method.'"

We can cultivate emotional well-being through developing our own personal practices. You might try the Carlos Method, a 10-10-10 practice of release and refuge, or you might explore your emotions through journaling, drawing, painting, dancing, or other creative projects. You can also practice naming emotions that arise with your physical sensations: When you feel a lump in your throat, you might note, "This is sadness." When you feel a stomachache before a presentation, "This is anxiety." Becoming familiar with the way your body relays emotional information puts you in touch with your emotional experience and gives you immediate feedback on your choices and actions as you go through your day. You can also practice stepping into Essence when you feel emotionally overwhelmed; this will help you develop emotional resilience and allow you to respond to the world with steadiness and compassion. Finally, you can practice expressing your emotions with "safe" people who are emotionally stable and healthy, so you become more comfortable expressing the full range of your feelings.

Emotions truly are the spice of life. Our life moments may be seasoned with love or hate, joy or sadness, self-assurance or fear, serenity or worry— sometimes, we can feel all these emotions in one day! Developing our emotional intelligence allows us to harness the power of these feelings to drive our life in the direction of a meaningful and fulfilling life. When we are no longer undone by fear or shame, we can take greater risks: We can pitch a bold idea to our colleagues, ask someone out for a date, or be the first one to volunteer for karaoke! Knowing how to work with anxiety, we can take giant steps into the unknown: We can make the decision to move in with our partner, apply to graduate school, or walk away from a job that has never served us. Comfortable with excitement and delight, we can be spontaneous and playful with our friends, give ourself permission to do that one wild and crazy thing we always wanted to do, or we can show up free and joyful in our lovemaking. And when we are peaceful with pain and loss, we can bring calm reassurance to a loved one who is sick or dying, or a friend as they grieve a loss. Life is seasoned with emotions. With emotional resilience, it all tastes great.

Social-Relational Domain
- The Social Realm -
The Freedom to Connect Joyfully

When you reflect on the best moments of your life, how would you describe them? Perhaps they involve special people, a favorite place, or a stunning vista. You might recall how you felt in the moment—peaceful, joyful, fully alive, a sense of belonging, or feeling at "home" in yourself. Chances are the best moments of your life involve *connection* to cherished people, animals, nature, the Divine, or yourself. For many of us, the deepest contentment arises when we feel close to someone or something.

Meaningful relationships enrich our life. Connected with our loved ones, we laugh harder, rest more deeply, take bigger risks, and live more vibrantly, often feeling a sense of completeness in the presence of our companions. Relationships are also supportive—our friends, family, and community help us carry our load in life, giving us a shoulder to lean on in times of difficulty. Relationships are also generative—we build better and greater creations when we play off each other's ideas, and many hands make for easier work. And our relationships help us evolve and adapt; it is others who cultivate our potential, open us to new worlds, and invite us to stretch beyond our habitual knowledge and patterns.

Without others, we could never realize our full potential, as no human develops in a vacuum. Through our encounters with the world, I have become "me," and you have become "you."

Successful relationships are built on a foundation of intimacy, empathy, collaboration, adaptability, and synergy. *Intimacy* is the ability to "show up" for relating. When we are open, curious, and interested in others, our encounters are fresh and stimulating, making for rich exchanges. *Empathy* allows us to understand others' experiences, engendering wisdom, care, and compassion as we relate to others. *Collaboration* is where "my intelligence" interacts with others' intelligence to unlock the genius of "our intelligence." Through a back and forth play of ideas and effort, we awaken new capacities that we would never manifest on our own. Our collaborations also boost *adaptability*. Together, we embody greater strength and stability, generate smarter coping strategies, and take turns resting and leading the charge, to persevere even in challenging situations. And when these collaborative efforts "synchronize," we experience the exhilaration of *synergy*. Moving and thinking as "one," we surrender our individualized "Me" to merge with the creative force of "We." In sync with others, we open a magic that reveals our true potential as human beings—riffing in a jam session, playing as "one mind" on a team, brainstorming with colleagues, or dancing as a group, we tune into something *more*, revealing the creative power of *One*.

Our relationships with the world are driven by internal relational "scripts"— the psychological beliefs and expectations we carry that govern how we relate to the world. For example, if we believe that all people are "untrustworthy," we will treat everyone with suspicion. If we believe "everyone is a friend until proven otherwise," we will treat everyone with friendliness. Our relational scripts also dictate how we relate to objects and the non-human world as well. Have you ever told a chair, "Move it!" or "Get out of my way!" Have you talked to trees, insects, animals, the weather, your washing machine, or planet Earth? What about God and the Universe? If you do talk to God, what kind of relationship do you have?

Are you pious... adoring...dismissive...demanding...terrified...friendly? Whether we know it or not, we are in relationship with the entire world.

The power of our relational scripts was shown to me when I was in graduate school, studying to be a psychotherapist. One day, a professor handed out copies of automobile insurance claims. As we read the reports, giggles rippled across the room, as each report was filled with startling excuses as to why the accidents occurred. The drivers wrote statements such as:

"The telephone pole jumped out of nowhere and hit my car."

"The pedestrian dove under my car, damaging my car."

"The little old lady wanted me to hit her because she didn't get out of the way."

And famously, "I didn't think the speed limit applied to me."

These drivers' psychological beliefs were projected onto the people and objects involved in the accidents, revealing the fears, contempt, and privilege that these drivers carried. When we are fearful, it can feel as if everything is out to get us, including telephone poles. When we are contemptuous, it is pedestrians who get in our way and are to blame for accidents. And when we live with a sense of entitlement, we believe that rules such as speed limits do not apply to us.

Where do these psychological beliefs and ideas come from? As it is with all our domains, our relational world is shaped by our early experience. If our childhood environment was loving and accepting, we came to *expect* that others would be loving and fair—if we spilt our milk as a young child and our mother kindly said, "Not to worry... Everyone spills milk at some point," and then she gently helped us clean it up, we learned that it's okay to make mistakes. Likewise, if our parents said, "I'm sorry," when they lost their cool, we learned about accountability and apologizing for missteps. But if our early environment was hostile, abusive, shaming, or neglectful, we came to expect the same from the world: If people reacted harshly to our mistakes, we learned to minimize or hide our transgressions. If the adults in our life were never accountable or didn't take responsibility for their behaviors—never said "I'm sorry," or "I was wrong"—we learned to avoid blame and project it onto others when we make mistakes. And if the people in our life were manipulative, we learned to be calculating in our social interactions. When we have been conditioned for surviving instead of thriving, our social behaviors can take on an "every man for himself" mentality where virtues such as truth, fairness, equality, kindness, accountability, and justice breakdown.

When we live in a personal world enshrouded by fears, wounds, and formations, we begin to see the world not *as it is*, but rather *as it was*, and act accordingly. We may watch a company softball game from the sidelines, wishing to join in, but decide against it, recalling the painful rejections we experienced in childhood when our peers didn't allow us to play their games. We may lean in for a hug with a friend and immediately brace, anticipating the coldness we felt in our father's steely hugs. We may initiate sexual play, only to shut it down the minute our partner responds, suddenly overwhelmed with memories of painful encounters. Anytime we act defensively or withdraw in our relationships, we can be sure formations are hampering our efforts to connect with others.

As you reflect on your Relational Domain, how do you relate to others? In what ways do you flourish in this domain? Perhaps, you are a true friend—reliable, caring. You may be a genuine extrovert; you love to make people laugh, you're easy to get along with, and you enjoy big gatherings and parties. Perhaps you are a great listener. Or you may enjoy taking care of others. Maybe you're great with animals and love connecting with Nature, or you deeply enjoy merging sensually with your partner.

In what ways do you struggle in this domain? You may be uncomfortable in large groups of people. Perhaps you feel awkward around children or authority figures. Maybe you're shy, or you struggle when communicating with others, or you can't get through a social event without alcohol because you're just too anxious around people. If you have been harmed through trauma, abuse, or neglect, you may no longer trust people, or you only feel comfortable when you are alone.

Finally, how do you relate to yourself? Are you kind to yourself? Do you speak to yourself with love and affection...with indifference...or harshly? Do you tell yourself, *Good Job!* Or are you more likely to say, *You should have done better!* Reflecting on your self-talk, where did you learn this? Are you imitating someone from your past? If you grew up with criticism and harsh judgment, you might take a moment to offer yourself some Loving Kindness. What you have learned relationally can be unlearned, and you can come home to your True Nature.

If we wish to change the way we relate to ourselves and the world, we can develop skills and attributes that promote healthy relating. To engage the world successfully, we need to:

- Understand the forces that shape our psychological beliefs about people and relationships.

- Recognize that people have different temperaments and relational styles, honoring the unique ways others "show up" in relationship.

- Clear our own limiting formations so we can see others *as they are*, without the distortions of our past.

- Develop our social skills so we may relate effectively, authentically, and kindly with others.

- Recognize the importance of family and community and take time to promote their cultivation in our life.

Connection is the bedrock of our human existence. Through our relationships we grow, evolve, and develop...we love, party, and play...we share ideas, recipes, and secrets, and unfold the power of "We." When we cultivate strong social relationships, not only does it enrich our lives, but we enrich the lives of others as well. When we share our wisdom, gifts, and skills effectively, we create a world where everyone thrives.

Different People, Different Styles

On a crisp fall day, I received a call from Jen, the middle school science teacher, asking if we could meet. I hadn't seen Jen for a year and as I listened to her on the phone, I found myself smiling as I recalled her sparkly tutu and bright energy. When she pranced into the office later that week, she had the same radiance, but now she walked taller, with a dancer's flow, and she had a real confidence about her. She took her seat, arranged the pillows just as she had in the past, then turned to me brightly.

"It's nice to see you again!"

I smiled warmly. "It's nice to see *you* again!" We took a few minutes for pleasantries, then she jumped in.

"So, my school's promoting STEAM education, you know—Science, Technology, Engineering, Art and Math—and I got picked to mentor a Destination Imagination team. DI organizes project-based STEAM challenges where kids can compete at the local level and winners can take it all the way to international events."

I smiled, warmly. "I'm familiar with Destination Imagination! My kids did it when they were younger."

"Well, then you know how much pressure there is—it's a pretty serious competition. And I want our kids to do well, but I've got an eclectic group. I've got to help them to gel as a team quickly, and I don't have all year to cultivate them, like I do in my classroom. I was hoping you might have some good ideas on how to create a team—*fast*."

I smiled. "I think it's great that you have a diverse group! That can be a real asset in a DI competition. Anytime you bring a group of people together—kids or adults—there'll always be a mix of temperaments; some people are strict, others are playful, there are rule makers and rule breakers, creators and builders, and there are leaders and followers. To build a successful team, you don't need everyone to be the same, they just need to be complementary."

> To build a successful team, you don't need everyone to be the same, they just need to be complementary.

Jen burst out laughing. "Yeah... Well, right now, the team doesn't look too complimentary! I've got little Einsteins...dreamers...the kid who keeps asking for breaks so he can go out and play basketball..."

I chuckled. "And yet, they all signed up for Destination Imagination! So, they must have an interest in learning and creating. Perhaps if you have a better understanding of their different temperaments, you can channel their strengths and bring them together as a team. When I work with people, I like to use a simple framework that illuminates how people show up in the world and interact with others. In my experience, I find that people primarily orient through their mind, their body, or their heart."

"For example, when I meet a person who's very analytical – let's imagine that they live primarily 'in their head' analyzing information, thinking about things, enjoying 'heady' subjects such as math, science, technology, or philosophy—that tells me that they are *mind-oriented*. As a group, these people express their Essence beautifully through their mind. They tend to be very structured and rational people; they love organizing data, working out problems, programming, or having long philosophical debates on their favorite topics. You'll often find them in 'thinking' jobs—computer processing, research, or jobs that require a lot of mental acuity such as authors, managers, professors, doctors, lawyers, or scientists. As children, these are the kids who can be very serious; they may be "bookworms," little scientists, mini professors, or they're the kid who likes to correct adults every chance they get."

Jen lit up. "I *definitely* have a couple of those kids in my group!"

"Great! They'll bring lots of structure and attention to the details of the project. Now, the second orientation involves those who live passionately through their body. Body-oriented folks express their Essence in amazing physical ways—they love sports, exercise classes, playing outdoors, dancing—anything that involves movement. They also love to express themselves through the body—they might be into fashion, or they love dressing up and going to parties, or they're bodybuilders. Often, they look amazing—they have a great sense of style and lots of cool clothes and accessories..."

"Like boas!" Jen was beaming. "I have tons of boas!"

"I imagine you do, in many different colors! Now lots of times, you'll find body-oriented people in physical jobs or jobs that have lots of activity. They may be landscapers, physical trainers, builders, dancers or entertainers, or business travelers. If do they have a desk job, they'll often move a lot, going around the office socializing with everyone, and right after work, they'll go for a run, take a dance class, or head to the gym. On weekends, you'll find them camping, boating, or climbing—anything involving fun and movement. These folks are always 'on the go' having big adventures, meeting new people, and living life large. As kids, these are the youngsters who can't wait to get outside for recess, and they tend to be very social; you'll find them organizing games or getting the other kids to try cool things."

Jen laughed. "I definitely have one of those in the group! He's always angling for a break so we can play a game. Funny...this orientation sounds a lot like me! I love dancing, cheering the kids on at school and getting students to do wild and crazy things."

"And yet, you're a science teacher!"

"Yeah, but I'm not one of those stuffy, serious science teachers, like my colleague Bruce. He's a 'stick in the mud.' I'm into science so I can blow stuff up!"

I laughed. "I imagine you're a very fun science teacher! Which actually brings up a good point. In truth, every human has all three orientations—mind, body, and heart—we are not just one "type;" it's just that we tend to live in our favorite corner, usually an arena where our domains shine most easily. For example, a mind-oriented person may be very caring, coming from their heart, but their care can often be of an analytic nature—if you're feeling lonely, they may come up with five plans on how you can make friends. A heart-oriented person may just sit down and give you a hug. To be successful in life, we want to be fluid and competent in all arenas, expressing ourselves equally in our mind, body and heart. You're pretty balanced in all the orientations, which helps you be successful, and yet you still have a favorite corner; you like to play in the body/movement arena. That's why you'll wear boas to a science fair."

Jen smiled. "Sparkly fun sells science!"

"Now, the third orientation is that of the heart. Heart-oriented people are intimate with everything. They love connecting with people, animals, the earth, nature, and they are very intimate with their projects—whether they're making art, creating whimsical gardens, collecting special rocks or shells, or caring for their knickknacks. Their Essence really shines when they're connecting with others, and they know how to 'show up' and be present. These folks are often very sweet and kind-hearted, and they're great listeners—with humans and the natural world. You'll often find them staring out a window, absorbed in the sky, the trees, or the sunlight...Standing still, savoring a breeze... Talking with animals... Or walking slowly and thoughtfully through a forest, connecting with everything around them. Since their days are spent absorbed in connection with the world, they can look a bit like dreamers, but they are simply engaged with the intimacy of the moment. As adults, you often find them in jobs that revolve around support or beauty—they may work as a nurse, a preschool teacher, an artist, or veterinarian. As children, these are the kids who enjoy having quiet tea parties with stuffed animals, putting Band-Aids on the family dog, and collecting pretty rocks and flowers to give as gifts."

Jen sighed dreamily. "There are two kids in the group who fit that description. They're such sweet kids...a bit on the quiet side. I'd love to draw them out more."

"If you offer them some kind gentleness, I'm sure you can draw them out of their shell. As I said earlier, we all have a favorite corner, but to be successful in life we want to be proficient equally in our mind, body and heart. As a mentor, you can foster more balanced functioning in your students by inviting them to step into their other corners. For instance, you might encourage your quiet heart-kids to lead a brainstorming session with the group—the more they do it, the more confident they'll become using their analytical skills."

Mind—Body—Heart

Where do you orient from most strongly—your mind, body, or heart? In other words, where do you experience the *most* joy? Do you love figuring things out...do you love being outdoors and moving your body...perhaps you thrive on being in connection with people, animals, or the world. Another way to think about it is, where is the first place you go to under stress? Do you immediately try to figure things out and fix things...do you take space to discharge stress...do you tend to freeze or collapse?

If you find yourself orienting predominantly from one corner, you can develop greater balance by cultivating your less developed corners. If you spend a lot of time in your head, make time to go for a walk, move your body, and do something that nourishes your heart. Each day, make sure that you do something that feeds your mind, body, *and* heart. When we cultivate all three orientations, we balance our own development and find healthy ways to connect with others.

Importantly, I wanted to impress upon Jen that we need all three orientations to have strong, successful groups. "Jen, your mind-oriented kids will be great organizers. And your body-oriented kids will bring lots of joy and creativity to the group. Your heart-kids will bring lots of warmth, thoughtfulness, and depth. The same holds true whether we're working with kids or adults in groups. When we understand the different orientations, and make room for their unique contributions, we create vibrant, thoughtful teams."

Jen paused, reflecting for a moment. "This all sounds good, but how do I get them to gel together?"

"One way to build team spirit is to help them 'see' each other. When people are seen for their gifts and wisdom, it creates great connection and empathy in a group. A good way to do this is to open some of your sessions by asking them to talk about their favorite passions. When

> When people are seen for their gifts and wisdom, it creates great connection and empathy in a group.

people talk about their passions, they light up, and their True Nature shines. A mind-oriented child will captivate the group with their Minecraft game or astronomy models. A body-oriented kid will enchant the group as they share how they rode their bike over a homemade obstacle course. And the heart-kids will bring out the warmth in the group as they talk about their dog, or how they cared for a hurt bird. Seeing each other clearly opens a joy and warmth that is contagious, creating a sense of unity and comradery."

Jen smiled. "I like that. Just imagining them doing that makes me feel the warmth and belonging."

"You can also create bonding through a game called *Common Ground*: Everyone stands in a circle, and you name a condition or event. Anyone who has experienced that event goes to the center of the circle. You can start with fun topics like, 'If you like ice cream, step into the middle.' You can also use examples related to their DI experience. For instance, you might say, "If you've ever built something, go to the middle.' Or 'If you've ever been in a play...' Or 'If you've ever felt nervous giving a presentation in front of a class...' With each question, the kids get to see what they have in common, which in turn, opens warmth and empathy between them."

Jen was smiling. "This is great! Can I get some paper, so I can write this down?"

"Of course!" I handed her a pen and pad of paper and waited as she made some notes.

When she was done, she looked up. "Okay, what do I do when they're stressed? They fall apart the moment things get stressful and heated."

"All groups struggle with stress—we see this even in adult groups, and with our families! Think of it this way, when the pressure's on, people most often retreat to their respective corners, and the three orientations have very different ways of handling tension."

"When mind-folks are stressed, they tend to go "up in their head" to grapple with the problem—they roll up their sleeves, start organizing and analyzing the situation, trying to get the problem resolved. Given this need to "hurry up and fix it," they can sometimes come across as abrupt, cold, or controlling. So, when the team's under stress, your mind-kids might become very 'intellectual' and start bossing everyone around."

"Body-oriented folks tend to move away from problems, often believing that things will 'work themselves out.' They 'take flight' to get away from the tension—they might make a joke, or change the subject... For example, if you confront them on an issue, they may choose that exact moment to get charming and start fawning over you and beguiling you, complementing you on your boas, to deflect attention off the problem. Or they might suggest that you go do a fun activity, asserting that the problem will work itself out if you 'take a break from it.' Other times, they might actually leave the room as in, "Let's talk about this when I get back from the gym.""

"Now, when heart-folks are stressed, they can freeze, collapse, or go into hiding—they may look like a deer in the headlights, collapse into tears, get sick, or suddenly become quiet and withdrawn. Given that these folks are heart-oriented, they feel everything strongly—they don't really have a filter between them and the world, so they need time to process and *feel* their way through the issue. When they're confronted with stressful problems, they need time to contemplate all the factors and utilize their intuition, so they're less 'strategic' in the thinking process. But in taking time to consider all the pieces, they often come up with very thoughtful, comprehensive insights that relate to the issue."

"These stress reactions are all variations on the *fight-flight/fawn-freeze* response. Mind-folks often fight the problem; body-folks tend to flee from the problem, and heart-folks freeze. Now of course, under big stress, we can experience all these responses. If you are caught in a burning building, you may run through all three reactions. But under daily stress, people tend to react in a way that is consistent with their orientation. So, when a group in under stress, everyone runs to their respective corner, making it's hard for the team to work together to create a successful resolution."

Jen leaned against the couch, resting her hands behind her head. "This makes total sense. As you're describing these reactions, I can think of lots of people who fit these descriptions—students...teachers I work with... even my principal! I've definitely seen the fight-flight-freeze response in my classroom—some kids challenge me, others try to get out of the work, and some kids shut down when the work gets hard. So, how do I get them back on track?"

"Well, if we can soften the stress and tension, most people will come out of their corner back into more balanced functioning. You can do a group exercise to relax the tension or take a break. And it helps to know how to calm each orientation. With mind-kids, they relax when they understand that they don't have to figure it all out on their own. For instance, you might say, 'Let's put our heads together. I'm sure we can find a solution if we work together,' or 'How can I help you?' With body-kids, it helps to remind them that they won't get stuck in this horrid, stressful space. You might say, "If we can stay with this just *a little* longer, I think we can find an answer and move on.' And heart-oriented kids love to be invited into connection: With these tender ones, you might say, 'Let's do this together,' or 'How can I support you?'"

Jen smiled. "I can definitely do that! Give me minute, I want to write this down." When she finished writing, she looked up eagerly. "What else do you have?"

I chuckled. "Basically, if we want to create successful interactions, it helps to be mindful of others' orientations. With mind-folks, it works best to meet them in the realms of thinking, processing, working, and figuring things out. Ask them what they *think* about things, instead of what they *feel* about them, and concentrate on data and facts. Also, they love to take a lot of space—that's how they think best—so don't take it personally when they're not being social. When you're relating with a body-oriented person, keep the energy light—go for a walk or add some movement, and ask them about their latest adventure. For them, freedom is the key to happiness, so give them lots of freedom. And when you're conversing with them, speak their language—use lots of movement and sports metaphors, phrases such as 'being in the zone' or 'hitting it out of the ballpark.' With heart-folks, they are happiest when they feel connected to others, so speak softly and gently, connecting with them through your heart. Ask them how they *feel* about things or invite them to share their favorite passions. When we meet people in the world they live in, they feel held, seen, and respected, and that goes a long way in creating successful relationships."

Jen looked happy and relieved. "Thanks! This gives me a lot to work with. Who knows? Maybe they'll work so well together, they'll create a masterpiece and take First Prize!"

* * *

When we understand the forces that shape relationships, we are empowered to act wisely in our social encounters, opening the door to sweeter connections, more joyful exchanges, and successful teamwork. Recognizing that our past influences our present interactions, we can center ourselves in empathy and compassion when things "go south" in our exchanges—people aren't trying to be difficult, they are caught up in old formations. When we have an appreciation for the *three orientations* (living primarily through our mind, body, or heart), we can relate to others skillfully, honoring their unique way of "showing up" in the world. When we recognize that people will retreat to their orientation "corners" in times of stress, we can wisely engage them to calm things down and not take their stress reactions personally.

When we understand our relational influences, we are also empowered to advance our own growth in the Social-Relational Domain. Seeing how our old relational stories sabotage our present relationships, we may be inspired to release our formations so we can rediscover the playful, joyful ease we had when we were younger. As we let go of our fears and expectations and center in Essence, we will find that it's much easier to be ourselves around others, and to be curious about others, sparking new opportunities for social connection.

When we recognize our own orientation (mind/body/heart), we can take pride in our unique expression and confidently ask others to honor our strengths and contributions. If we find ourselves stuck in one orientation, we can make a conscious effort to cultivate our other corners so we can live more fully, opening the door to our True Nature, and we can have fun doing it! If you are a mind-oriented person, you might ask your body-oriented sister to take you paddle boarding. If you are a body-oriented person, you can ask your heart-oriented child to lead you on a hike, taking time to look at all the pretty rocks and flowers as you make fairy homes. If you are a shy, quiet, heart-oriented person, you might ask your active, body-oriented friend to take you to their dance class.

As we develop our corners, it opens us to our True Nature, inspiring us to engage in fresh social encounters. We can say "Yes!" to that party invitation, confident that we can create a good time wherever we are. We can join a club, a walking group, or meet-up at the dog park, open to meeting new people. We can say, "Hello!" to our grumpy neighbor, sure that they will appreciate our kindness even if they can't quite take in the warmth. And we can invite our co-workers for lunch or coffee, happy to expand our friendship circle.

When we bring an open heart, engagement, and warmth to our social encounters, we embody the Success Traits—we are thoughtful, kind, and observant; we are inclusive, lighthearted, and inviting; we are warm, respectful, and

> When we bring an open heart, engagement, and warmth to our social encounters, we embody the Success Traits

generous. And in this joyful presence, others begin to relax and be authentic when they are around us. Feeling safe and welcomed, they can express their true passions and their heart freely. When we create a space where others feel safe and accepted, the ripples create truly successful communities all around us. In the ease of joyful connection, everyone and everything is invited into our circle, where True Success can happen for all. And that makes for a truly successful world.

If you want to go far, go together.
—African Proverb

Social-Relational Domain
- Intimate Relationships -
The Freedom to Love Without Fear

When it comes to the Social-Relational realm, we all know that there is a big difference between our social relationships and intimate relationships. Many of us can be "socially on" and gracious when we are out in the world—we talk to our colleagues at work, go to dinner with friends, or enjoy a weekend game with some of our sports friends. Out and about in the social world, we may feel relatively successful. But when it comes to our intimate relationships, many of us feel like we are floundering. Why is that?

Intimate partnerships are challenging because they present a paradox: Romantic relationships are meant to be a refuge, a place where we rest, recharge, be ourselves, and have fun, and yet many of us find intimate relationships stressful. At times, the stress we experience comes from outside our relationship. When we have to contend with external stressors such as work issues, raising children, tending to our extended family, dealing with racial or cultural pressures, or coping with financial difficulties, we may have little energy left for connecting with our beloved. Anytime we feel burdened or don't have enough space for self-care, it's hard to show up for others.

But while all couples contend with external forces, ultimately our partnerships are defined by internal forces—our capacity for intimacy and healthy relating. If we are relaxed and at ease in our togetherness, we can rest and feel nourished in our partnership. But for many of us, intimate connection is not a "refuge." Instead, we feel stressed in the presence of our partner: We may feel a certain pressure to be "on," to be "good," or make ourself "desirable" to our partner—mandates that feel very different from *rest, recharge, and have fun.* And when we add sex into the equation, things can get even more complicated. If we are uncomfortable with sex or the appearance of our body, we may freeze or contract anytime our partner touches us or steps in for connection. Other times, we may feel "turned off" by something our partner said or did, unable to rekindle our interest in connecting. And some of us yearn to rest deeply in our partnerships, only to find ourselves with a partner who isn't interested in tender connection. We reach out, and they recoil, or look at us as if we're the enemy, leaving us feeling confused, apprehensive, and lonely. And some of us find ourselves living in abusive or unhealthy relationships, never able to relax or let our guard down. This paradox— being told to rest in relationship when it may not actually feel restful—is why intimate relationships can feel so exhausting. The romantic scripts we see in movies and media don't line up with our personal experience.

Why is it so hard to relax and "show up" in our partnerships? As it is in all our domains, our psychological beliefs and old memories hold the key to our relational patterns. If our early experiences were filled with acceptance and love, we will find it easier to rest in relationship. But most of us have experienced some pain, hurt, and fear in the relational realm. Our relational scripts were written when we were very young, at a time when our tender hearts were unguarded and sensitive. In that innocence, the first rejections, attacks, and betrayals we experienced with others were the hardest hitting, spiraling us into feelings of sadness, disillusionment, and bewilderment, making it hard for us to relax and trust people. In the rawness of our first wounds, many of us decided to hide in our broom closet, believing that if we could keep our heart separate from the world, no one could hurt us. On the outside, we might smile and look as if we're engaged in our relationships, but our heart has been tucked away in a safe place for a very long time.

Discovering Your Relational Scripts

To better understand your inner relational world, make some quiet time to write your answers to these prompts: *Love* means... *Marriage* means... *Commitment* means... *Receiving love* means... *Giving love* means... *Taking help from others* means... *Letting others shine* means... *Caring for others* means... *Sharing* means... *Sex* means... *Touch* means... *Snuggling* means... *Kissing* means... *Taking care of others means... Being generous* means... These are some of the psychological stories that are defining your Relational Domain.

If any of these meanings open fear, discomfort, or pain, take a moment for some self-care. You might offer yourself some Loving Kindness or go outside to take in some beauty. If you struggle with intimate relationships, know that it is possible to release your pain, on your own, or with a trusted therapist. When you release your painful relational stories, you can create new connections that support joyful, healthy relating.

If we want to have successful relationships and embody the full freedom of our True Nature, we need an open, loving heart, for True Success is built on an ability to live and love without fear. With a strong, unbounded heart, we can give *and* receive love, resting deeply in our intimate relationships, nourished and replenished through connection with our beloved. When we live with a trusting heart, we pave the way for fulfilling fun and healthy togetherness. This is what Barb and Rob were hoping to find when they came to see me for couples therapy.

We had only been working together for a few weeks when they stomped into my office one evening and plopped down at opposite ends of the couch. Barb looked out the window, tapping her foot. Rob folded his arms and turned away from her.

Warmly, I said, "Hello! So, what's going on this evening? You both look stressed."

Instantly, they began arguing about their parenting, Barb accusing Rob of being lazy, while Rob countered that Barb was a "bitch."

To shift the energy, I let out a long, unwinding sigh, cuing them to relax. "Okay, let's take a moment and unbraid this." Each of them threw me a look of disdain as they rolled their eyes in unison.

"You're never going to change him," Barb snapped. "I've been telling him what to do for years and he never listens."

Rob sneered. "Yeah, well maybe it's because you're always bitching at me, telling me what to do!"

Over the past weeks, it had become clear that their entrenched viewpoints were arising out of their orientations. Barb is a strong mind-oriented person who works as a college administrator. She loves spreadsheets, data, and organization and she likes things to be orderly and predictable. As Rob could attest, she brings her orientation straight into their home life—Barb wants a clean house, homework done, and she meticulously schedules their kid's extracurricular activities and practice times. In contrast, Rob is a body-oriented "dude" who is a gifted musician. He works at the same college in the music department, where he's a beloved professor and inspiring leader of various bands. Rob isn't concerned with organization and tasks; he's more into passionate living and having fun.

While they may seem like opposites, Barb and Rob share a number of common passions. They are both devoted to their kids, and they love music, particularly Jazz. As part of their summer vacations, they attend at least one jazz festival every year. True to form, Rob loves tracking down the festivals and collecting the tour dates of great musicians, while Barb enjoys organizing their travel plans. Back in the days when they had few worries and lots of time for concerts, things were a lot smoother in their marriage. But as they settled down and started a family, the stress of maintaining a stable home proved to be overwhelming. Juggling the high demands of parenting and work, each had retreated to their respective corners—Barb fixated on organizing the family and offering enriching experiences, while Rob advocated for laid-back family time, sure that this was the best thing for their kids.

As I listened to them arguing, it was clear that they were stuck in their gatekeepers, neither of them offering warmth or understanding to each other. I could see that Barb had the upper hand in this argument, feeling confident in her role as the authority, while Rob was beginning to unravel as Barb demeaned every point he made. To bring a little more balance into the exchange, I asked Rob to share his thoughts.

"Rob, help me understand what upsets you about Barb's behavior."

Sounding like a young child, he whined, "She's always telling me what to do!"

"That's because you never do anything!" Barb barked.

I gently asked Barb to sit back so Rob could finish his thoughts. She huffed dramatically and flopped against the couch, folding her arms, resuming her stare out the window.

I turned back to Rob. "So, she tells you what to do all the time. Anything else?" Rob's narrowed his eyes, "Yeah, she hides out in parenting! She acts like she's doing it all for us, but we don't want to do half the stuff she comes up with—the sport teams, art lessons, karate lessons, clean the house—we just want to hang out as a family, but she's always trying to improve us."

Barb exploded. "I'm not trying to IMPROVE anyone!! I'm giving our kids a chance to have a NORMAL childhood!!! Did you ever think of that?! And YOU'RE not helping!!!"

Rob gave me a smug look. "Do you see what I live with?!"

Turning to Barb, I said calmly, "I can see that this is a hot topic. And I want you to know that I hear you—that you want to give your kids a *normal* childhood." Barb's eyes welled and she nodded, looking relieved that I heard her.

* * *

Intimate relationships are filled with lots of landmines and gatekeepers—one wrong move and we can find ourselves in messy, explosive mayhem. When things get "hot" in a relational exchange, I take it as a sign that it's time to do some "deep listening." I could sense that Rob felt undermined by Barb's bossiness, and I believed Barb when she screamed that she was not trying to "improve" her kids, that she only wanted them to have a "normal" life.

After reassuring Barb that I had heard her, I turned to Rob. "I can see that you're really mad about Barb 'bossing you around.' Would it be okay if we look at this for a moment?" He groaned in frustration, then nodded. Having his consent, I invited him to close his eyes so he could mindfully notice his inner experience.

"You've said more than a few times that Barb 'bosses you around.' What comes up for you when she 'bosses' you around—what does it *mean* when she's being bossy?"

He reflected a moment, then flinched. His eyes shot open; his voice filled with bitterness. "It means *she's in charge of me.* She's acting just like my mom!"

"I'm glad you see that. Now, can you go back inside and be with that experience?"

He closed his eyes again. A moment later he grumbled, "It's just like when I was a kid. My mom was always bossing me and my brother around. All she cared about was having a clean house. She never played with us, we never did anything fun as a family, and it was always just chores, chores, chores! When you care more about how your house looks rather than if your kids are happy, that's messed up." On the other side of the couch, Barb was looking surprised and a little intrigued by Rob's explanation of the issue.

"So, when Barb bosses you around, it reminds you of how your mom focused on chores and she never spent any fun time with you?" Rob nodded. He opened his eyes, looking very young and forlorn, like a sad little boy. From the other side of the couch, Barb quietly murmured,

"I'm sorry your mom never played with you. She's still self-absorbed, she never spends time with us or the kids."

Rob nodded, looking down at his hands. "Yeah..." We had made it past the gatekeepers. Now we were in tender territory.

Just as it is in other domains, the psychological meanings and beliefs we carry from our past color our relational scripts. We look at our partner and think, *she acts just like my mother*. Our beloved might touch us, and we think, *You just want sex, just like every man I've ever dated*. Our partner offers to help us in the kitchen, and we think, *You think I can't cook a meal? You're just like my father*. Often, we're not even aware of these comparisons, but if we listen to the stories we are telling ourselves about our partner, we can hear the themes from our past.

The scripts and formations we bring to intimate relationships are some of the most potent and compelling because they were formed in our most vulnerable moments—those times when we were naïve, innocent, and undefended in our first connections. If we have lots of positive memories of being held on our parents' lap, encouraged in our schoolwork, and cheered on at our sporting events, we learned to lean in and rest with others. But if we have lots of memories of being yelled at, shamed for our mistakes, or laughed at when we offered our love or gifts, it knocked the wind out of our joy and loving. Add to this the pains of life, such as caring for an injured bird and watching it die, and our heart reeled in pain and bewilderment: *Why do things die when I love them?!* These early painful experiences can crush our confidence and trust in the world, leaving us quivering in our broom closet.

If we want to flourish in our intimate relationships, we need to heal our wounds and step out of our broom closet, for only then can we engage with others to live and love fully. As I sat across from Rob, it was clear that he needed to release his pained little boy; otherwise, it would be hard for him to show up as an "adult" partner in this marriage. I invited Rob to close his eyes and connect with the little boy again. When he was mindfully settled, I asked the boy what would feel nourishing. Rob didn't hesitate; the boy wanted a new mommy, one who would adore him and play with him. I invited Rob to imagine that mommy and the nourishment that would come with the new relationship, then guided him to release the formation and rest in Essence. In Essence, Rob saw that his mother's self-absorption was driven by an anxious belief that she wasn't "good enough." Believing that a pristine house would impress her neighbors, she drove her boys to achieve perfection, but the clean house never brought happiness. As Barb mentioned, to this day, Rob's mom is still self-centered, focusing on her own needs.

With the release of the little boy, Rob was grounded and centered in his adult identity. When he opened his eyes, he somberly turned to Barb. "I love you and I want us to work this out. But I'm clear that I won't live the way we've been living. I want to be with someone who loves me and the kids and wants to spend time with us, not just doing chores and going to practices."

Barb nodded, but she looked unsettled. I got the feeling Rob had never set a boundary like this. Quietly, Barb responded, "I want us to work it out too. And I'm sorry for bossing you around. I love you, and you and the kids should have fun. I'll work on less scheduling."

Rob shook his head, not buying her deflection. "I'm not looking for *less scheduling*, I'm looking for more *connection*." Barb nodded, but she looked hesitant. I could see that Rob's request was making her uncomfortable. We would need to attend to that discomfort if they were going to move forward. Sensing their commitment to each other, I was hopeful that they could do the work that would bring back the joy and connection they had once known.

Healing Our Relational Trauma

[Note: This section contains references to trauma]

I didn't see Barb and Rob for a few weeks as they were busy with mid-terms. When they returned, they looked stressed. Barb was quiet, but Rob got straight to it.

"I helped with the kids, I didn't make her my 'mom,' and I even made her favorite dinner. But as soon as I try to connect with her, she gets all distant and cold! I tried to put my arm around her when we were watching a movie, and she actually pulled away. The other day, I offered her a kiss as she was leaving for work, and she acted like she was too busy, but she wasn't too busy to answer a text from her friend, Margi before heading out the door! And we haven't had sex for... a long time now."

I glanced at Barb to see her response, noting that she looked frozen. Gently, I asked, "Barb, do you want to say anything about this?"

She looked as if she wanted to cry or run away. She sat up and in a tight voice said, "He did help a lot. And I'm very appreciative of that."

Rob flared, "Well, you don't act appreciative!"

Gently, I intervened, "Rob, let's give this a chance. Remember how I asked Barb to sit back when you were exploring your pain?"

He looked at me, surprised. "She's in pain?" He turned to Barb. "Are you in pain?" She looked at him, unable to say anything, her eyes wide.

Softly, I asked, "Rob, can you see Barb's fear?"

Looking puzzled, he kept his eyes on her face. When he didn't answer me, I took the moment to check in with Barb. "Is it okay to explore this?"

She nodded. Haltingly, she said to Rob, "I've been afraid...all week." She shivered and turned to me with tears, "I can't do this right now." Unsure what was happening, Rob was now looking at Barb with care and concern.

To offer Barb some safety, I handed her some tissues and invited her to slowly breathe out the tension and fear she was experiencing. When she looked a little more settled, I asked, "Is it okay to work with this fear today?"

She nodded. "Yes," she said, dabbing her eyes. "I want us to be closer. That's why we're here."

I turned to Rob. "Would you be willing to support Barb's healing today? As we work, she might hit a rough spot and say something that is painful for you to hear. I need you to be clear that this isn't about you."

He nodded, then turned to Barb. "I'm here for you." Barb smiled timidly. "Thanks... I think."

To help bring Barb's fear into focus, I asked if they would be willing to do a simple exercise. With their agreement, I gave the instructions. "Rob, I'd like you to turn to Barb and say, 'I love you.' And Barb, I'd like you to notice what comes up in your mind, body or heart when he says that. No judgment about what happens, we're just exploring this."

Rob looked at me, incredulous. "That's it?"

I smiled reassuringly. "That's it." He turned to Barb, and with genuine love and warmth in his voice, he said, "I love you."

And Barb froze.

Softly, I asked, "So, as Rob says, 'I love you,' what's happening in your body?" Barb looked intently at Rob, not saying a word. I asked again. "Barb, what's happening right now?"

She took a shaky breath. "I feel panicky... My heart's racing...and I want to get away."

To offer some safety, I made a suggestion. "If you like, you can place your hand on your racing heart and see if that helps." Barb placed her hand on her heart and closed her eyes. After a few deep breaths, her body began to relax. Softly, I asked, "What are you noticing now?"

She let out a long exhale. "I feel better...calmer."

"I'm glad that feels better. If your hand could talk, what would it be saying to your heart?"

Barb took in a deep calming breath. "It's saying, 'You're okay... You're okay...'"

"That sounds very comforting. If you take a moment to sense into this calm, soothing voice, is it familiar to you?"

She was quiet a moment, then she softly whispered, "It feels like Essence." With the revelation, she sighed softly, and her shoulders relaxed.

"As you rest in Essence's comforting, would it be okay to keep working?" She nodded, so I asked Rob to say the phrase again.

"I love you." Barb flinched, only this time, she held her seat.

"What's happening now, Barb?" Staring intently at Rob, she drew in a shaky breath. "I feel scared...hot...like I want to cry..." Tearing up, she kept her focus on Rob.

"Can you say something about the tears?"

"It's my dad." She was trembling.

"Do you want to say more about that? You don't have to if you don't want to."

We sat in tender silence a moment, then Barb whispered, "I hate my dad." She pressed her hand into her heart and breathed deeply, all the while staring at Rob. I could see that Rob wanted to reach out and comfort her, but I knew that if a memory of abuse was coming up, any touch could feel violating, so I offered him a different job.

"Rob, can you support Barb by staying present with her and supporting her with deep listening?"

He nodded. "Sure, I can be here for Barb." He turned to Barb with an air of strength and loving support.

We sat silently, allowing Barb to pace the unfolding. "He used to come into my room at night... And in the morning, he would say, "I love you." She cringed, as tears streamed down her face. To Rob, she said, "I can't have you say that. It's too much."

Rob nodded with tears in his eyes. "I knew he hurt you, but I didn't know about 'I love you.' I won't say it. I don't want to hurt you."

Knowing that it wouldn't work to forbid the words, 'I love you' in a marriage, I turned to Barb. "Would it be okay to work with this memory?" She nodded, looking very much like a little girl. "Um...yeah. I don't like it. I wish it would go away."

"Can you close your eyes and feel into the memory? You can keep your hand on your heart." She closed her eyes and pressed her hand into her heart. Gently, I asked, "How old are you in this memory?"

"Eight. I'm in my bedroom, curled up on my bed. He's not there."

"I'm glad he's not there. I imagine she's pretty hurt and scared, so let's create some safety. As you touch in with this hurt little girl, can you also sense Essence in the background?" She was silent a moment, then nodded.

"Good. Can you feel its calm, safe peace?" Another nod. "You can breathe into that peace and ease and rest there for a moment." After a few breaths, her shoulders relaxed, and her breathing became steady.

Now as you're anchored in Essence, I'd like you to notice something... Is Essence eight-years-old?" She shook her head.

"Is Essence scared?" Again, no.

"Wonderful. Now I'd like you to notice something very important. Even though this abuse happened, does Essence feel *violated?*"

She was quiet a moment. Then in a relieved voice she said, "No. It feels safe and peaceful."

"Barb, this is very important to see—*to know for yourself*—that the deepest part of you has never been harmed by your father. His actions never touched your Essence. At your core, you are safe, whole, and free. Your essential nature has never been harmed by this world, let this sink in." I gave her a moment to absorb the revelation. "What's it like to know that the deepest part of you is absolutely safe and okay?"

Barb let out a long sigh as she relaxed back into the couch. "I feel like I'm not broken."

Gently, I concurred. "You were never broken; through the trauma you lost connection with your Essence, but now, you're home again. Take a moment to sense into that... *Your Essence has never been broken.*" I watched as she breathed deeply, her chest opening and expanding. "If you like, you can breathe this gentle peace of Essence over to the little girl so she can sense this calm and safety." I waited a moment, then quietly asked, "How's the little girl feeling now?"

Quietly, she said, "She feels better, a lot less scared."

With the little girl feeling safer, it was time now to release her. I asked the eight-year-old what would feel safe and nurturing to her. With a relieved sigh, Barb said, "She wants to be in a meadow with some baby animals, where there's no people and no one can hurt her."

"That sounds like a perfect place for her to feel safe." I invited Barb to rest in Essence and then guided her to release the little girl. With her hands over her heart, she breathed slowly, her body shaking and trembling as the energy of the trauma released.

"How are you doing?" I asked.

With her eyes closed, she murmured, "I'm okay, but I feel really hot."

"That makes sense. When we release pain or trauma, sometimes the energy is released as heat. If you like, you can imagine yourself in a big, open, natural space—a beach, a meadow, or a mountaintop—give this heat and energy lots of space as it rises out of your body."

She drew in a few steady breaths, exhaling slowly. "That feels better."

When she looked more settled, I invited her to name two qualities that were present within her now that the trauma had released. In a relaxed voice, she said, "I feel expansive and safe."

"If you like, you can take a moment to breathe this expansiveness and feeling of safety throughout your body, saturating your cells with peace and ease."

When Barb opened her eyes, she looked relaxed, soft, and serene. Turning to Rob, she said warmly, "Thank you for supporting me." Rob smiled back. "You're welcome." In that moment, they were truly connected, resting in their love as they looked intently in each other's eyes.

We were sitting quietly in the warm silence, when Barb turned to me. "Thank you. I feel really calm. I haven't felt this safe in years."

There would be other sessions around the abuse, but with each release, Barb became lighter, freer, and more playful. As Barb and Rob continued to release their fearful formations, they began to settle into a warm, trusting connection. Essence became their relational refuge— They danced in Essence, snuggled in Essence, and made love in Essence, creating an intimacy and tenderness they had not known before. Barb and Rob no longer needed their gatekeepers to feel safe; they felt safe with each other.

The summer after I ended my work with them, I saw Barb and Rob at a concert. They were holding hands, dancing in front of the stage, laughing and hugging. When they saw me, they ran over to offer hellos. "It's great to see you!" Barb exclaimed. "We love this band! Rob found them a few months ago and we've been following them ever since."

Rob nodded, beaming. "We're doing great! We're getting along... having fun together..." He gestured around him. "Look, no kids! We're actually having a date!"

I laughed. "Good for you! I hope you have a sweet evening filled with love and fun!"

Barb leaned closer to Rob. "Oh, we will! Life's pretty sweet these days!"

What Does That Mean to You?

The next time that you get in a squabble with a loved one, take a moment to ask them, "What does that mean to you?" For example, "What did it mean to you when I was late?" "What did it mean when I didn't return your call right away?" "What did it mean to you when I said that I thought you could've handled that better?" Inquiring into the meaning of words and actions gets to the heart of the matter very quickly, allowing us to address any misunderstandings.

This also works when we get upset with our loved ones. Asking ourselves, What does it mean when they _____ (are late...look at their phone while I'm talking to them...cut me off, mid-sentence?), will give you instant feedback on the psychological beliefs and stories that are being stirred up in you. To calm yourself, offer yourself some Loving Kindness or release the formation that is activated. When we understand the meanings that are driving our relationships, we are empowered to heal our wounds, allowing us to foster loving, healthy connections.

---

* * *

Our journey to loving without fear begins when we realize that it is possible to heal our relational trauma. With self-compassion and the right practices, we can release our old relational pain to reawaken our loving, happy heart. Our healing truly flourishes when we engage our Essence to make an amazing discovery: The traumas we've experienced have never harmed or violated our essential nature. Essence has never been touched by rejection, abuse, shame, or hatred. Essence has never felt afraid, bitter, broken, or timid. At our deepest level, we are, and have always been healthy, whole, safe, peaceful, and strong. Knowing that deep down we are truly "okay" opens a feeling of peace and safety that brings back our calm and sense of trust.

In the meantime, as we are working to release our trauma, we can get a taste of this deep calm by utilizing *Taking Care Gestures*, a variation on a Hakomi technique I learned during my mindfulness psychotherapy training. When Barb was overcome by her anxiety and racing heart, I gently invited her to place her hand on her heart. As she mindfully breathed out her tension while holding her chest, she instantly felt relief, reporting that she felt "much better." I then asked, "If your hand could talk to your heart, what would it be saying?" to which she replied, "It's saying, 'You're okay... You're okay...'" The soothing words and tender holding eased her anxiety, making her feel safe.

Taking Care Gestures can take many forms. Like Barb, when we feel pain or fear in our body, we can gently hold the pained area in compassionate warm support. We might also take up soothing movements such as rocking, rubbing our arms, humming, or wrapping ourselves in a blanket. As we rest in these comforting gestures, it helps to ask, "If this _____ (rocking...holding ...warm blanket) could talk, what would it be saying?" The calming words that we hear within us are a soothing balm, quieting our fears and discomfort, helping us relax.

Over the years as I've employed these calming gestures with clients, I've often asked them to sense into the "source" of the calming voice. Initially, many tell me that it feels like the gentle voice of a kind parent. But upon deepening into their experience, they often shift their perspective, reporting that it is their own Essence in the form of a comforting parent. The beauty in this revelation is that they see for themselves that they have a deep source of comfort *within* them. With the continued release of fearful formations, Essence is what remains—the calm, strong heart of their True Nature.

As we discover our inner safety and release pained, traumatized formations, our fear and anxiety begin to subside, quelling the adrenaline and cortisol that have been coursing through our body, sometimes for years. In the calming of these neurochemicals, we come home to our natural mind and body and in our healing, a new life opens. We begin to sleep better. Aches and pains connected to the holding of tension begin to disappear. We may feel less anxious or no longer have panic attacks. We might lose weight. We may find that there is less drama in our life. We begin to relax around people, especially our partner. And if we've been in unhealthy relationships, we find that we no longer are attracted to unhealthy dynamics; we find ourselves seeking out more stable companions. If we have avoided intimate relationships due to our trauma, with enough release, we may find ourselves becoming interested in exploring romantic connections again.

Coming home to the natural mind and body of our True Nature, we begin to breathe easier and unlock a new delight borne from freedom. Like Barb, we may become more joyful and playful. We may find ourselves smiling more. We might begin to notice more beauty in the world, inspiring us to relax more deeply in our happy heart. With all this joy and ease, we may someday leap out of our broom closet, excited to give our beloveds a big hug!

> When we see our partner *as they are*, no longer confusing them with the people of our past, we can enjoy fresh exchanges that build trust, friendship, and joyful connection.

True Success in the Social-Relational Domain invites deeper connection with our loved ones. When we see our partner *as they are*, no longer confusing them with the people of our past, we can enjoy fresh exchanges that build trust, friendship, and joyful connection. When we recognize people's orientations (mind, body, heart), we can foster the expression of True Nature in all our relationships: We can invite our partners to play in our corner, and we can play in their favorite corner, eliciting a sparkle and joy that enlivens our connection. When we begin living with an open loving heart, our intimacy with the world flourishes, deepening the richness of our life as we create truly successful, truly loving connection.

The Spiritual Domain
The Freedom to Explore the Mystery

Have you ever found yourself wondering...*Where did I come from? What is this "aliveness" that I feel...is it energy...my soul...an expression of God? What happens when I die? Does it matter what I do in this life, or are there no consequences to my actions?* It is natural to ponder such questions for we are born with a capacity to contemplate the abstract, to reflect on things that lie beyond our everyday existence and the world we experience with our five senses. Mesmerized by a sunset, we may feel connected to something *more*. Talking with a stranger, we may marvel at the serendipitous discovery that we both love the same small chapel in a European town. Hiking through a forest, we may feel "one" with everything. Praying at our mosque, temple, or church, we may feel held by an all-encompassing Divine Love. Such experiences excite us and intrigue us as they expand our sense of self and our understanding of Life and the Universe. This wish to comprehend "the world beyond our world" is a central theme in the Spiritual Domain.

While we may not name it as such, all of us have been on a spiritual journey of some kind or another. For many of us, it began with the teachings of our parents' religion and how our parents related (or didn't) to the mysteries of the Universe. As we got older, we likely delved into our own explorations of God and different religions, or we looked to philosophy and metaphysics, hoping to resolve our spiritual and existential questions. And if we've ever experienced a moment when we felt "one" with the Universe, had a spiritual vision, heard an otherworldly voice of guidance, or sensed a Divine Presence, we may feel certain that there is *something more* beyond our everyday human existence. For some of us, simply getting in touch with Essence feels like landing in our "soul." In the same manner, if we've never had an otherworldly experience, we might conclude that it's all "hogwash"—where's the proof? Through our spiritual experiences, we make conclusions about life and existence that shape our view of the Universe and how we live in it.

It is hard to resist the "spiritual impulse" for it is hardwired into our brain—literally. Neuroscientists have pinpointed regions in the brain that correlate directly with spiritual beliefs and experiences. In one Yale University study using functional magnetic resonance imaging (fMRI), researchers asked people of diverse spiritual traditions to describe their profound spiritual experiences. Irrespective of race, creed, culture, or gender, the participants uniformly recounted feelings of oneness, a connection to "unseen elements," a sense of timelessness, boundlessness, and transcendence, all while the fMRI scanner recorded parallel brain patterns. It was also noted that spiritual experiences could occur without religiosity—some participants recalled powerful spiritual encounters that transpired outdoors in nature, during ordinary daily activities, or while meditating. This study, and others like it, reveal that while we may hold different spiritual beliefs and practice different spiritual traditions, *our transcendent experiences are the same.*

But while our spiritual experiences may be similar, our interpretations of them vary widely. Imagine for a moment that an individual senses a "presence" or "energy" surrounding them or near them. This type of experience has been reported by many people of differing beliefs, and may serve as a powerful or transformative event, and yet how they contextualize it will be shaped by their beliefs, religion, personal history, and cultural conditioning. A person devoted to Christianity may sense the energy as the presence of Mary or Jesus, a follower of Hinduism may experience it as the blessing of Krishna, while a person grieving the death of a loved one may sense it as the soul of their dearly beloved. Similarly, a scientist who is agnostic may describe the event as an electromagnetic charge, and while they may be filled with wonder at this "miracle" of the Universe, they may have no need to attribute the event to a divine source.

Given our different understandings and interpretations of transcendent experiences, I find it helpful to make a distinction between spirituality and religion. *Spirituality*, as I am defining it, refers to our personal explorations into the nature of Life, the supernatural, or whatever we might call Ultimate Reality in our attempt to connect with deeper dimensions of our existence. Spirituality can include metaphysical experiences, contact with a sense of the Divine, moments of intuition or "hunches," and other experiences that illuminate "the world behind our world." The interpretations we give to spiritual events are our own *personal meanings* derived from our understanding of the world, regardless of what others believe or tell us to believe. In this context, spirituality is very private—it is the personal meanings we make about God and the Universe in our heart and mind that go on to shape our consciousness, morals, and our behavior as we move through the world.

In contrast, *religion* is a codified set of beliefs and practices based on historical traditions of particular cultures. Religions often focus on belief in a Divine Source, offering teachings and practices such as prayers, prostrations, meditations, chants, and ceremonies as forms of worship to deepen the participant's connection with the Divine. Religions can also define social norms, demarcating what is "good" and "evil," and describe what will happen in the afterlife given our behavior on Earth. For example, to receive the rewards of a favorable afterlife, many religions stipulate that their followers must worship God in the ways endorsed by that religion, as well as make choices that benefit not only oneself, but others as well.

But even with these guidelines, many religious followers carry their own spiritual interpretations of the doctrines. As a child, I remember being told at my Catholic school that if a person was not a "Christian," they could not go to heaven. Distressed, I asked my mother, who was a devout Catholic, if this was true. "What if someone never hears about Jesus, but they're still a good person and they do good things...will they never go to Heaven?" She reflected a moment then said, "If someone has never heard of Jesus and they are good, they will go to Heaven. God knows the goodness of their heart." As I got older, I was surprised to find that despite calling themselves Catholics, my parents held a number of spiritual beliefs that differed from the ones offered by the Church.

In a similar way, a belief in God does not necessitate belonging to a religion. In a recent Pew survey, 95 percent of Americans reported that they believe in a Divine Source, yet only 27 percent attend weekly religious services. The reasons given for not partaking in religious services were varied. Some cited outdated doctrines that no longer align with our current knowledge of the world. Others were turned off by what feels like the "business" of religion. And many reported that they were offended by religious divisiveness and the sexual abuse perpetrated by clergy members.

Others turn away from their religion for more personal reasons. I have worked with many people who have stepped away from their church or temple after experiencing personal harm from those who purportedly subscribe to religious adherence. As one client told me, "It's hard to 'honor your father and mother' when you live in an abusive home. Those teachings just don't work for me." Others have shared that they were sexually or emotionally abused by religious elders. And some were shunned by their family or religious community for being gay or for choosing to have children outside of marriage.

When we experience personal harm or distress in religious settings, sometimes our only option is to walk away, a decision that doesn't come without heartache. Separating from our religious community, we may feel lost, untethered, or bitter. We may struggle with sadness or an inner restlessness, unable to feel "at home" in ourselves, in the world, or with God. We may feel despondent, believing that God has somehow abandoned us. In our quest to find a spiritual home, sometimes we encounter what appears to be the very opposite.

As a child, I was enamored with all things spiritual. I regularly talked to God, I loved hearing spiritual stories, and I relished saying my prayers at bedtime. But when I was a teenager, my boundless enthusiasm for all things spiritual, turned to cynicism when my family endured several tragedies, culminating in the death of my mother when I was seventeen. As my mother lay in the hospital, I recited all my Catholic prayers, begging God to save her life. I asked the saints and angels to help, believing what I had been told about miracles. I reminded God of all the ways I had tried to be good, convinced that goodness was rewarded with divine favor. But the religious promises I had been given in childhood didn't materialize, and when my mother died, I felt lost, abandoned by God and my Catholicism. In protest, I stopped going to church. I was still interested in God, but not in the God of my Catholic upbringing.

Even when we struggle in the Spiritual Domain, it is hard to ignore the spiritual impulse. When we are in conflict with our religion, our spiritual beacon may actually become stronger, compelling us to find a new spiritual path. Following the death of my mother, I felt compelled to find spiritual solace, driven on by an inner restlessness that yearned for a spiritual "home" that would ease my pain and help me understand why my mother had to die. Over the next decade, I took up yoga, practiced martial arts, shared in friends' religious services, dabbled in various kinds of meditation, visited different churches and temples, and got certified in mindfulness-based psychotherapy. With each tradition, I gathered many spiritual "gems" that gave me solace and peace, but I was still searching for *something*.

My experience is not so different from others. In the Pew survey on religion, many participants disclosed that while they had lost interest in religiosity, they were still maintaining a spiritual practice. Fifty-five percent of adults reported that they pray daily, while 40 percent reported that they meditate at least once a week. The spiritual impulse is strong, urging us to find a sanctuary where our heart and mind can rest in tranquility as we access teachings that inspire meaningful, compassionate living.

While I was grateful for the spiritual traditions I encountered, I still struggled to find the spiritual sustenance I was looking for. In my meditations, I couldn't sit quietly, and as soon as I got off the cushion, I slipped right into my old habits of fear, anger, and anxiety. *Why couldn't I be peaceful and loving?* As often happens, the answer came masked in a crisis. Sometimes our spiritual journey takes a turn into what St. John of the Cross called the *Dark Night of the Soul.*

When I was in my thirties, I was in a skiing accident, and later that year diagnosed with thyroid cancer. It was a difficult time that brought up lots of fear and anxiety as I faced the pain, treatments, and fear of death that engulfed me that year. In my unraveling, I saw the limits of my psychotherapy training and my spiritual practices were not holding me; clearly, I needed "something more." Gratefully, a friend introduced me to a spiritual teacher who instructed me in deep mindfulness and concentration practices that allowed me to transform my pain and fear into my first experiences of Essence. When we encounter the Dark Night of the Soul, we often encounter spiritual supports that help us open to deeper realms.

As I delved into these deeper practices, I encountered spiritual experiences that transformed my mind and heart. I began to enjoy long moments of peace and tranquility that quieted the inner restlessness and anxiety I had felt most of my life. Inspired by mindfulness practice, I immersed myself in Buddhist meditation and long spiritual retreats. I also became interested in how psychology, Essence, and spirituality can interface to bring greater health and spiritual depth. In my meditations, I began to notice how mental formations from the past brought up anxiety that hindered my spiritual explorations. If I released these formations, I landed in the vast ease of Essence. Heartened by this experience, I began releasing mental formations as part of my daily practice, and over time, the peace and ease of my Natural Mind was revealed. I no longer needed to use concentration practices to find peace; it was simply what remained when the formations were gone. As I came to rely on Essence more, I discovered the joy, love, and wisdom of what I call my True Nature.

It was during this time that I was invited to serve on a teaching council at a Buddhist meditation center. Serving on the council brought me a wonderful opportunity to deepen my practice and delve into mindfulness teaching. For eight years, I took joy in teaching classes on meditation, mindful parenting, mindfulness 12-Step work, and compassionate living. I found that the more I gave myself over to my spiritual practice, the more I softened and loved, landing in a spiritual "home" that continues to feed my heart and guide me in compassionate living.

When we delve into the Spiritual Domain, we open the door to an expansive, richer life—one that opens our hearts and minds through connection with the magic and splendor of "that which lies behind our world." Whether we come to our spiritual explorations through religion, science, inquiry, prayer, meditation, ceremony, or rituals, we have an opportunity to expand our consciousness, our heart, and our sense of who we ultimately are. When we know ourselves spiritually, we live in the world more fully and kindly for we recognize the entire Universe as "home," and *that* meaning inspires us to draw upon the Success Traits in all our encounters with the world.

Barriers to Spiritual Development

Dave and I met when I was hired as a consultant for an at-risk youth agency where he was the director. Dave was a bear of a man, a big cantankerous Texan. He tolerated no B.S., spoke straight to the point, and he relished fighting any person or bureaucracy that threatened the well-being of "his kids." But beneath all his bluster, Dave had a huge heart. He loved the kids who came to the agency, and no matter what they were facing—run-ins with the law, poverty, abuse, abandonment, learning struggles, or school expulsion—he was always in their corner, helping them secure a better life.

After working together for several years, I moved onto other work, and Dave and I lost touch. I still got "Dave updates" from various colleagues—he was still "fighting the good fight," advocating for kids and developing community programs, so I was surprised when I got a call from him asking if we could meet "professionally." When he walked in the door, he had his usual grouch on, looking over my office as if he was assessing my credentials. "Nice plants," he said wryly as he sat down.

"Thanks! Nice to see you again. So, what brings you here?"

He growled, "I don't know if this is the right place...but you always had a good attitude in the work, so I thought maybe you could help me out. I can't say this to many people, but I'm sick of my job."

"I can understand that. You have a hard job. What are you sick of?"

He sighed heavily. "I started working with kids when I was in my twenties, thinking I was going to make a difference in the world. But I've been at this for twenty-five years and nothing's changed: Kids are still struggling, and the politicians don't 'give a shit' enough to make the changes these kids need in order to thrive and do well in life. Every day kids pour into my office, and I do what I can, but the need is endless. You know how it is; you work with people's problems. How do you keep doing it? Don't you get sick and tired of it all?"

I nodded sympathetically. "I do have moments when I get discouraged, but when I feel overwhelmed, I find it helps to lean into something bigger..."

"Yeah, well I don't have 'something bigger,'" he said, sarcastically. "And if you're talking about God, don't go there. I work with these kids every day and I don't see God doing much for them."

I was beginning to understand why Dave was so exhausted. Denying that there was anything "bigger than him" was leaving him vulnerable to overwhelm, despair, and emptiness.

If Dave was struggling in the Spiritual Domain, what was "holding" him? Curious, I asked, "So what supports you when you're giving so much in this work?"

He sneered. "I eat bureaucrats for lunch!" Then sinking again, he said, "I don't know...my wife Shanna cooks a good dinner... I have a beer, watch a little television." He sighed loudly. "Shanna goes to church, and she prays for me; she says I need it. She tries to get me to go to church but..."

"But what?"

"I never got much out of church; it was all pretty rote for me. And besides..." He rubbed his face, exhaling a tired sigh. He was close to naming something, so I waited. He grumbled, then continued. "When I was twenty-three, just out of college, I got hired as a tutor for the kids over on the Southside. I was working with this kid, Jules...he was really smart. He had it rough, but he had big dreams! For two years we worked together: He got his grades up, applied to college, and he got accepted! He even got a scholarship! But then..." Dave winced. "The fuckin' kid got *shot*." His voice quivered. "I begged God to help him... to keep him alive. I prayed harder for Jules than I have ever prayed for anything in my life. Jules was a great kid, and he fuckin' died! So, yeah, I'm out there fighting for my kids every day and I don't need God or anything "bigger" to help me!"

Softly, I said, "I'm sorry about Jules. It's hard when we care so much about a kid, and it doesn't go well."

He grunted. "Yeah..."

"So, you've been doing it all on your own, but now you're exhausted."

He tossed his head in disgust. "Yeah..."

Seeing how tired and overwhelmed Dave was, I knew it was important to attend to his burnout before he could rest in "something bigger." I talked to him about doing some release work at our next session so we could ease his stress and tension. After explaining a little more about what we'd be doing, Dave warmed up to the idea.

"Okay, that sounds good. I didn't think *this* was going to happen. I thought you were going to tell me to take an anger management class."

I smiled. "I find that when we release our tension, our stress and anger often go away."

Looking a little less beaten down, Dave smiled. "That makes sense. Well, I gotta get back to work." He stood up to leave. "Text me some times when we can meet, and we'll set something up." As he walked out the door, he looked a little lighter.

Our Spiritual Psychology

When it comes to developing a healthy spiritual life, it helps to look at the psychological beliefs and attitudes we bring to spiritual matters, for our beliefs greatly impact our spiritual experience. Like Dave, many of us bring our personal stories and philosophies into the spiritual realm—if we believe in God, we have our reasons; if we don't believe in God, we have our reasons—either way, our psychological beliefs are influencing our engagement with *the Mystery*.

The beliefs we carry in the Spiritual Domain are some of the most fervent and passionate for they are concerned with our very safety and existence. We want to believe that we are *held by something bigger* that cares for us and our world. We want to believe that we and our loved ones will *live on forever*. We want to believe that *it matters* that we were here, and that *we are good*, living out a just and honorable life. We want to believe that we are following the one *true religion*, or that we know *the truth about reality*. If life throws any of these beliefs into doubt, like Dave, we may spiral into existential crisis, feeling as if we've been abandoned or our very existence is threatened: *Why didn't God help me? Maybe there isn't a God. What's going to happen to me when I die? Will I go to Heaven? Will I be reincarnated into a Hell realm?*

With so much at stake, we take our spiritual beliefs very seriously. Consequently, when our beliefs are challenged, our gatekeepers often come out swinging, hurling threats, insults, and sometimes knives at anyone who threatens our spiritual view. This is why Dave growled, "Don't go there!" when I asked about resting in "something bigger." It's also why we don't discuss religion and spirituality at social gatherings— the topic is just too "hot" for calm reasonable discussions.

The spiritual beliefs we carry about God, religion, and the Cosmos are strongly shaped by our personal experiences and our Psychological Domain. Do you recall the insurance claims that I discussed in the

Relational Domain? In that chapter, I pointed out that our psychological beliefs are projected onto *everything*: telephone poles, pedestrians, and the world at large. That "everything" includes God, the Universe, and religion. Given the power of psychology, we cannot help but relate to God or *The Mystery* through the lens of our past experiences and conditioning. If we were raised to feel safe, cherished, and secure in the world, we likely expect the same from the Universe. If we were shamed, abandoned, made to feel unworthy, or terrorized, we likely expect the same when we encounter powerful figures, particularly God and other spiritual authorities. In another example, we may publicly share a common belief that the Divine is all-loving and forgiving, yet if we have lived in a less-than-loving environment, we may fear that it is not so for "me." *Perhaps I'm unworthy of God's love and compassion.* The assumptions we make about Divine love are greatly influenced by the psychological beliefs we carry about our own lovability.

Our life experiences also influence our attitudes concerning other people's spiritual traditions. If we were raised to be trusting and curious about different cultures and traditions, we will likely honor others' spiritual paths and religions. But if we were raised to be exclusive or untrusting of other religions, we may feel suspicious anytime we encounter a religious tradition that is different from our own, no matter how loving and inclusive it is. Like all things in the human world, we see the Universe and other spiritual traditions, not as they are, *but as we are.*

Years ago, I witnessed this phenomenon during a camping trip with some friends. One evening, as the dinner plates were cleared and the sun was setting, a friend suggested that we get our sleeping bags to lie out under the night sky. When we placed our bags on the warm desert ground, the sky above us was deep indigo—vast, quiet, and still. We were lying in the dark for some time when a voice broke the silence, "What if there's nothing out there and we're all alone..." A few moments later, another voice, "What if a comet comes out of nowhere and hits us..." Then another, "I like to think God is watching over us..." And another, "Maybe God isn't real. Maybe it's just a story we tell ourselves because we're afraid of death." Then a disgruntled voice said, "Maybe we're all just star dust and there's no point to any of this." Knowing my friends' histories, I could see how their thoughts about "the Void" perfectly matched their childhood experiences. I was hearing everyone's past projected onto *The Mystery*.

A few months later I was walking with a friend, who happens to be a priest and a psychologist, when I mentioned the camping incident and remarked that many people seem to struggle with a fear of God. He listened intently then thoughtfully remarked, "Most people think they have a clear vision of God, when in reality, they have confused God with some past authority figure, usually their parents. If they've had harsh parents, they tend to envision God as harsh. If they had judgmental parents, they likely see God as judgmental. It's sad, really. As a priest, I'm always trying to help people encounter the Divine as it is, not as they fear it to be."

Our ideas on God and spirituality are also influenced by other factors such as our mental health. When we are mentally stable, our spiritual beliefs and practices tend to mirror our well-being. But if we suffer from psychological disturbances, carry toxic fears, or struggle with mental anguish, our mind may twist the practices, beliefs, and doctrines of spiritual traditions into unhealthy versions as we attempt to relieve our pain. All abuses of power and sexuality in spiritual and religious circles are borne of such mental instability. This is why it is so important to attend to our fears and anxieties; whether we know it or not, our fears are impacting our spiritual beliefs.

As we engage in spiritual practice, it can benefit us to examine the beliefs and mindsets we bring to our practice. For example, we might engage in spiritual practice primarily as a source of solace, asking the Divine to calm us or fix our world. We may engage spiritual practice with child-like formations asking God, the ultimate grown-up, to save us. If we release our formations and anchor ourselves in Essence—grounding in its calm, clear-seeing, and sense of safety—we may no longer identify with the inner child and as such, we may not need God to "parent" us and make everything "all better." Instead, we may find a maturity and strength that helps us feel fulfilled, allowing us to step into spiritual service. With Essence, we may also experience a composure and clarity that can ground us, helping us open more fully to our spiritual tradition to receive teachings and insights that lead to a loving, wise, compassionate life.

Exploring Your Spiritual Beliefs

When you have some quiet time, take a moment to reflect on your spiritual beliefs.

What beliefs or experiences from your past have shaped your relationship with Divinity or the Mystery? Is the spiritual realm a source of solace and reverence? Is it burdened by difficulty?

If you struggle with spiritual issues, you might take a moment to offer yourself some Loving Kindness. Compassionate care can be a great offering in our healing and renewal.

Developing a Healthy Spiritual Path

Dave and I began to meet weekly and Dave took to the work like a fish to water. He released his formations around Jules's death and rediscovered the compassion that initially fed his work. He also discovered that he *loved* resting in Essence. In Essence, Dave found a refuge that he had never known, something bigger than "Dave Inc." and it didn't require him to believe in anything outside his own experience. He was so enamored with his practice that he kept a set of blankets and pillows at his office so he could release his stress before going home each evening. "This is the best thing I've ever done," he told me. "I just lay on the couch for twenty minutes, let all the stress and anger rise out of my body, then I'm good to go. A lot of times, I just rest in Essence and feel tension rising out of my body - I don't even know what's leaving - I just feel heat and tension bubbling out! I'm feeling a lot lighter these days—the jackasses aren't getting to me as much, and I don't need a beer every night to relax." As

Dave was discovering, Essence is a wonderful refuge, full of intelligence and nourishment and he was now navigating his days with more ease, compassion, and patience, making him a kinder, more adaptive "Dave."

As our sessions progressed, Dave began to realize that Essence wasn't just a refuge for him, but it was a source of deep compassion. At one point we explored how Essence would respond to different scenarios.

"As you rest in Essence, imagine there's a kid yelling and kicking things in your office. How does Essence respond to him?"

"I feel compassion. Essence sees that he's in pain and I feel this impulse to help him."

"And if Essence sees someone who has hurt you? Perhaps someone from your past..."

Dave exhaled slowly. "That would be my brother...there's compassion...but also a lot of clarity about him. He was pretty mean to me when we were kids, and these days he's doing a lot of drugs. With Essence, I feel loving toward him, but I'm really clear that I shouldn't connect with him right now. Maybe someday..."

Seeing the compassionate nature of Essence sparked an interest in spiritual matters for Dave. One day, he spontaneously blurted, "Look, I'm not into any namby-pamby stuff, but if I was looking into what you're calling the Spiritual Domain, what would you suggest?"

I smiled, kindly. "Well, spirituality is a personal practice. I find it works best if you listen to your own heart. Of course, you could read some books on different religions and check out some churches or temples. There's also yoga...nature practices..." Dave cut me off. "I like that one—nature. I like camping."

"Nature is a wonderful place to connect with the spiritual part of you. You could begin by connecting to Essence when you're out in nature, and I'm sure you can find some books on meditating in nature or other outdoor traditions." He nodded, satisfied with my suggestion.

As it turned out, Dave loved his outdoor practice. He began meditating in nature and he practiced embodying Essence while hiking, sitting on mountain tops, standing in waterfalls, breathing in forest scents, and lying down in meadows. Following a trip back home to Texas and Big Bend National Park, he announced, "The outdoors is definitely my church. When I'm in Essence out there, I'm I touch with *something bigger*; just like you talked about." By following his heart, Dave was opening to a bigger reality, expanding his consciousness and shifting his understanding of the world.

A few months later, Dave arrived for his session looking as if the heavens had opened to him. "This really weird thing happened, and I want to tell you about it. Shanna and I were at Red Rocks this weekend— you know, that outdoor concert venue outside of Denver. Anyway, I was leaning back in my seat, looking into the night sky listening to the music and breathing Essence...when all of a sudden, the music went *through* me. I wasn't 'hearing' music...it was *in* me. And then I felt like *I was the music* floating through the air! It was like there was no 'Dave' for a moment, just *music!* It was a cool experience, but then I got scared. And all of a sudden, I was back to being 'Dave.'"

Familiar with the experience, I smiled reassuringly. "It sounds like you had an experience of *expansiveness* and what is often called 'groundlessness.' Sometimes when we are deeply relaxed and fully open to the present moment, whether in prayer, meditation, or doing ceremonies, we can have spiritual openings. Just as you experienced 'being' the music, we might feel the expansiveness of the Universe, or have a moment where we feel connected to *everything*. Some people experience being filled with Divine Love, or they sense the Universe as 'One Consciousness.' It's natural to feel unsettled when we first have these expansive experiences; at times, we may feel a bit panicked or a sense of vertigo when it happens, but once you get comfortable with expansiveness, it can be quite enlivening: We relax, let go of our stories, and just *be*...and as our tension and familiar orientation fall away, we begin to sense the world and ourselves in a new way."

"What's important to know is that you don't have to be afraid of these experiences. If it happens again, *relax*...and let yourself open to it. When we contract around expansive experiences it can feel unpleasant, so it's best to relax; you might even imagine yourself resting in a river valley or wide natural space—just as we do in our release work when things get too 'big" or groundless. And if you ever feel overwhelmed, you can always step back into Essence and ask, 'Is Essence scared of this?' In the same way that Essence doesn't get overwhelmed or scared by life events, it doesn't get overwhelmed by spiritual openings either. It remains calm and peaceful, watching spiritual events unfold with serene interest."

"Now that you've had this experience, I'm curious, how do you understand yourself and the world at this point?"

Dave reflected a moment. "I guess it made me feel like I'm part of something bigger. I asked Shanna if this kind of thing ever happened to her. She told me that she feels it in church sometimes—the music and prayer carry her some place. But she said it was hard to explain."

I nodded. "Many people have a hard time putting words to their spiritual experiences, and yet they leave us with an inner certainty that there's *something more* going on beyond our everyday existence, even if we can't describe it. When our consciousness expands, it expands our world, often leaving us feeling more connected to the Universe. I'm glad both of you are experiencing these openings, you'll have to see where they take you."

Dave's inner discoveries were definitely taking him in a new direction. He and Shanna were enjoying a new connection, sharing conversations about God and spirituality. Eager to share their spiritual unfolding, they decided to look for some retreats that offered a spiritual focus, eventually settling on an organization that offered "back to the land" retreats— simple camping with a focus on spiritual exploration led by respected spiritual teachers of different traditions. On their retreats they found that listening to birdsongs while meditating and taking "sacred walks" in meadows brought a pleasant ease that made it easier for them to open to a sense of scared presence, and their shared experiences were bringing them closer together.

As Dave continued his unfolding into "something bigger," he began embodying more of his True Nature and much of his "roughness" was fading away—I only saw it now and again when big losses occurred, such as when the city administrators cut a youth program that offered afterschool tutoring. On that autumn day, Dave and his "gatekeepers" stormed City Hall—barging into offices, swearing profusely, he blasted the bureaucrats. When he came to his session that week, he told me that his tantrum didn't last long; he was quick to notice his gatekeepers and quick to release them, admittedly, after spewing a few colorful words. "Those fuckers are lucky I do release work and I'm committed to a spiritual practice!" he said adamantly. "Your work is actually saving lives in this city; they should put you on a retainer."

By the time the holiday season arrived, Dave was back in good spirits and feeling spiritual, so much so that he decided to go with Shanna to her church for Christmas celebrations. When I saw him again, he had a sweet, knowing smile on his face. "There was music, chanting, incense, the whole nine yards... We were doing this long call and response thing, where the priest calls out a line and the congregation follows with a response—we did the same phrase over and over. As I was doing it, I closed my eyes and just let the words wash over me as I repeated the phrase, when all of a sudden, I felt the 'Presence' that I feel when I'm outdoors. I just opened to it as I said the response over and over, sinking into this peace. When the bell rang, I opened my eyes and... *I was connected to everyone in the room.* I just stood there crying. I couldn't speak... I couldn't move. It was as if I could see the *Essence* of everything, and *everything was made of Love*—the people, the building... I felt so *alive.*" He closed his eyes, remembering the moment. When he opened them again, they were wet with gratitude.

"Finding Essence and connecting with this 'Presence' has changed my life. You know, I've loved more in the last five months than I have in the last fifty-five years of my life. The more I open to a spiritual life, the more I understand that I'm connected to *everything.*" He lingered a moment. "And being connected to everything, makes me care about everything."

I grinned. "Even bureaucrats?!"

Dave choked on his laugh. "Oh shit! Yeah, I guess...even bureaucrats!"

We laughed a moment, then curious, I asked, "Do you believe this 'Presence' that's permeating your life is *God?*"

He grinned. "For me, it is. But it's not the God I grew up with. It feels more like what I would call a *Presence of Love.* I'm starting to think that the world is made from Love. This might sound real 'woo-woo,' but I feel like I was born to love."

I smiled. "I think everyone in this town knows that! You were just the last guy to figure it out."

He chuckled. "Damn! And here I thought I was a hard ass!"

* * *

When we delve into the Spiritual Domain and experience the non-physical aspects of our existence such as Essence and Divinity, we step far beyond the limits of "Me Inc." Engaging with "something bigger," we become "bigger." Experiencing an expansiveness of consciousness, we sense our interconnectedness with all things. Tapping into Divine Love, we are transformed in our body, heart, and mind. The more we deepen into *the Mystery,* the more we are healed and nourished by the web of life, and in our renewal, we come to realize that everything is sacred and precious. Strangers on the street feel like family. The tree we walk by on our way to work feels like a precious friend. When we see a bug on our windowsill, we greet it with a warm "Hello!" and gently put it outside. And when tragedy strikes, in our community or across the world, we are moved to compassion for "they" are "us."

When we avail ourselves to the mysteries of the Universe, we touch into a collective wisdom that inspires True Success. When we sense into "perennial wisdom," the recognition of our shared existence, it opens feelings of empathy and belonging that inspire compassion, integrity, and a desire to live a meaningful, principled life—the very qualities that engender the Success Traits. In the Spiritual Domain, we awaken qualities that make us kinder, more generous, caring, and responsive, emulating the loving care of true spiritual people. We need only to look to spiritual leaders such as Rev. Desmond Tutu, Mother Teresa, Amma, Martin

Luther King, Eckhart Tolle, the Dalai Lama, or Thich Nhat Hanh to see how a clear, calm heart can make a difference in the world. For many of us, the spiritual journey is the apex of our human existence. When we realize our True Nature and see the world with spiritually awakened eyes, we can't help but live a kinder, more meaningful, successful life.

What does True Success look like in the Spiritual Domain? It is the airport employee who plans his work break each day so he can reverently face Makkah to offer Fajr prayer at dawn. It is the grandmother who gets up early to attend morning mass to offer prayers for her family and the world. It is the Sikh community extending langar into neighborhoods to feed those who are hungry. It is the family who says grace before their meals and prayers before bed. It is the Jewish family gathering for Chanukah to celebrate and remember the importance of Light and freedom. It is the countless clergy who support their communities with spiritual teachings, prayers, and ceremonies in good times, and in bad. And it is Neil deGrasse Tyson and the production team of *Cosmos*, opening our hearts and minds to the unfathomable magnificence of this great Universe.

When we open ourselves to *the Mystery*, we cannot help but be transformed. Touching into the expansive awe, wonder, and peace of "that which lies behind" our everyday world, whether through religion, science, prayers, meditation, or ceremony, brings us home to a Presence that feels like our *deepest nature*. Whatever form of spiritual inquiry you embrace, may you find the transformation, peace, and understanding that awakens your heart and inspires you to live a joyous, compassionate life.

The Integrative Domain
The Freedom to Express Our True Nature

Have you ever made a lasagna? If so, then you know that there is a lot that goes into it. You have to prepare the sauce, cook the noodles, break out the ricotta, slice up some mozzarella, grate the parmesan, cook the meat or veggies, and add seasoning—onion, garlic, basil, oregano, parsley, and a little sugar to temper the sauce. Once you pull the ingredients together, it's time to layer the dish: Cover the bottom of the pan with sauce, place a layer of noodles, spoon in some ricotta with veggies or meat, place the mozzarella slices, add more sauce, generously sprinkle the parmesan, then repeat, adding layers until the pan is filled.

At this point in the process, you have a heavy pan filled with the right ingredients, but you don't have lasagna. Pop it in the oven for an hour, and as the ingredients blend together, they become a delicious dish. When you open the oven and take out the pan, *Bellissimo! It's Lasagna!*

Lasagna is the result of a process of *integration*. Separate, distinct elements join together under the right conditions to become a unified whole, an entity that is "more than the sum of its parts." You can put wet noodles, sauce, and cheese in a pan, but that doesn't make it lasagna. It takes the right ingredients, heated at the right temperature for the right amount of time to spark the alchemy that fuses the components into a luscious pasta dish. As any chef knows, perfect integration is the magic element in culinary art.

A healthy, successful human is the result of a similar process—the integration of our Lifeforce, our Essence, and the elements of each domain fuse together in a magical masterpiece that makes "you" and "me." Through the alchemy of integration, the individual domains—physical, cognitive, emotional, social, spiritual—are united, creating a unique individual who is "more than the sum of their parts."

To create successful integration in ourselves, we need the right elements and conditions:

- Healthy functioning in each of our domains
- Flowing interdependence between our domains
- A wholistic sense of self that embraces all the domains as an expression of "me."

Successful integration begins with healthy domains. Just as it is with lasagna, the quality of our "ingredients" determines how well our integration will turn out. If any domain is lacking or underdeveloped, our overall success will be compromised. To have healthy integration, we need a well-fed body, clear cognitive processing, balanced psychological beliefs, healthy relational scripts, and wholesome spiritual beliefs. If one of our domains is "off," let's imagine that we have low blood sugar, our functioning can be compromised across our domains; our emotions may become erratic or "cranky," we may become psychologically unbalanced, and our thinking and processing can be impaired. For this reason, successful integration requires a level of well-being and competence in all our domains.

Successful integration also relies on the supportive interdependence of our domains. It takes all our domains to execute the actions and choices of our life. For instance, to engage in deep spiritual practice, we need a healthy body, a strong brain, balanced biochemicals, stable emotions, and a healthy internal relational script in order to maintain our concentration and prayer during dedicated practice. Likewise, effective athleticism is built on the moment-to-moment flow of biochemicals, brain functioning, emotional regulation, and relational skills as we run up the field and throw the ball to our teammate.

This isn't to say that all our domains have to be perfectly developed. If we do have domains that are compromised, we can still achieve healthy integration through engaging secondary supports. The great theoretical physicist Stephen Hawking was unable to walk or speak, yet his use of an electronic wheelchair and a voice device allowed him to travel the world, meet with colleagues, and give lectures that allowed him to convey his brilliant insights in science. Healthy integration can arise both through the development and mutual support of our domains.

When we come to appreciate that all our domains are part of us and integral to our functioning, it opens a new sense of who we are and what it means to live successfully. No longer identified with just one or two domains such as, "I'm the smart one," or "I'm the pretty one," possibilities begin to emerge. If we are physically healthy, cognitively adaptive, psychologically balanced, emotionally strong, relationally engaged, and spiritually open, how might we live? Recognizing that we are much more than "pretty," we might take the lead in supporting a passionate cause. Seeing beyond our brilliant athleticism, we might look for a programming job or go back to school. Recognizing that we have lots to offer beyond our amazing engineering skills, we might host a meditation group, or create a profile on a meet-up app in order to meet new friends. When we realize that we are a capable, gifted human being, supported by all our domains, we can choose to embrace a wider, more interesting life.

Once we have decided on a new endeavor, we need to take steps to bring our aspirations to fruition. We begin by releasing any limiting fears that clash with our dream: If we don't think that we are "good enough" to attain our goal, we release that formation. Once we are free of our fears and doubts, we get training to develop our domains so we will be successful. Finally, the process of integration requires time for "marinating" or "cooking." Just as lasagna needs to bake in the oven for an hour at the right temperature to fuse into a scrumptious dish, we require time to study, practice, reflect, and integrate our new skills and knowledge in order to grow and evolve. If you are a student, you need time to study and digest the new material and skills you are learning. If you are an "empty nester," you need time to slow down, reflect, and plan the kind of life you want now that your children are gone. If you are a musician, you need time to integrate hours of practice and study in order to become proficient.

From a biological standpoint, this "marinating" and "cooking" gives our brain time to wire itself for new functioning. As Daniel Siegel points out in his Mindsight approach to personal growth, separate functions (i.e. different domains), become linked as we expand synaptic connection—the more we focus attention on an endeavor (studying or practicing), the more neural connections are made, making us more proficient in our new pursuit. Our first "lasagnas" might not turn out great, but over time we can improve our performance, building a competence that helps us achieve the right results. For instance, with practice, a musician can learn how to play more complex pieces with improved flow and precision. Integration takes time, so it requires patience. Becoming a healthy, successful person doesn't happen overnight.

When we integrate Essence into our domains, every room in our castle lights up, unleashing our True Nature, and the power to live a vibrant, successful life. The integrative functioning of our True Nature is our superpower—when all our domains are aligned and humming, we are strong, wise, joyous, and passionate; our potential can fully unfold, expressing who we are *meant* to be. In the Integrative Domain, we experience the freedom of being our full self; joyous, confident, and empowered, we are the ones who make our dreams come true.

In the Integrative Domain, we experience the freedom of being our full self.

Heeding the Call of Our True Nature

One morning my phone rang early, before my usual office hours. When I answered, I heard the sweet, familiar voice of Clarise. I hadn't heard from Clarise since she had graduated from college four years before.

"It's so nice to hear from you!" I said.

"It has been a long time," Clarise said with a nervous laugh. "Um… I was wondering if I could make an appointment. I imagine you're busy, but I could really use your help."

"Of course! Is there something specific you want to work on?"

"It's kind of complicated," she stammered. "I can tell you about it when I come in." We arranged to meet later that week. When I hung up the phone, I was smiling, happily anticipated our reunion.

When I opened the door to my waiting room, I barely recognized Clarise. The college kid I had known a few years before had blossomed into a striking woman. With her hair cut short and her professional attire, she looked like a lawyer. But when our eyes met, the college girl sprang to life, and she rushed at me for a hug. "Oh, I've missed you so much! I'm so glad you could meet with me!" After a long moment, she stepped back, tears in her eyes.

I smiled, touched by our mutual sense of connection. "Look at you… all grown up! You're a woman now! I am so happy to see you!"

We took a few minutes to settle in, talking about the weather and a new salad bar she had just tried for lunch. And when the moment seemed right, I asked, "So why are you here today?"

She took a big breath and let out a loud sigh. "I'm feeling pretty stuck. I'm not sure what to do with my life and I thought maybe you could help."

"Are you dealing with a particular problem?"

"No—and that's the problem! 'Technically' everything's great. I have a good job—I work as a medical secretary in the ER, and I make good money. Things are good in my life but…something's 'off.' I feel restless and edgy, and it's starting to get worse. I'm starting to feel claustrophobic."

I nodded warmly. "Well, I'm sure we can figure it out. Why don't we start with a little overview, that way we can see if there's a particular area that's not in alignment. Would you be open to looking at the Seven Domains? Do you remember the domains?"

Her eyes widened. "Oh, yeah! I still think about them... I try to make sure they're all okay."

"Great! So, how are you doing in the Physical Domain? Any health issues or physical problems?"

"No, I'm really healthy. I eat well, go for a run a few times a week, I love yoga... I'm good with my body."

"Well, you look pretty healthy! Okay, so how's the Cognitive Domain... Any difficulties with thinking, memory..."

She shook her head. "No. I do really well in that area. I read tons of books and I use my brain *a lot* at work."

"How's your Spiritual Domain?"

"That's good too. Like I said, I'm really into yoga. I use it as a physical practice but it's also my spiritual practice. I study with a teacher in Boulder, she has amazing presence. She talks a lot about 'scared embodiment;' it's opened a whole new world for me."

"She sounds like a great teacher! What about the Social-Relational Domain?"

"It's good. I don't have a partner or anything, but I have an amazing group of girlfriends. We're like a pack—we do everything together. We like to travel and have tons of fun. I don't want a committed relationship right now; I feel like my twenties is 'me' time." She paused, looking sure of herself. "Yeah, I'm just trying to figure out who I am and what I'm supposed to do with my life." But as she said these words, her energy dropped.

"And how are you doing emotionally? You said that you felt 'stuck.'"

Clarise frowned. "Yeah, I'm not doing so well in that domain. I've been vacillating between discouragement and anxiety. Sometimes, I feel this sad yearning...like I'm supposed to be living a different life. And then

I feel panicky, thinking I'm supposed to be doing something important or meaningful, but I don't even know what that is."

Clarise was clearly at a turning point in her life. If she could slow down and listen deeply to herself, I knew she would arrive at an integration that would open a new phase in her life.

Kindly, I said, "So, you have this idea that you should be doing something more meaningful... That could definitely make you feel stuck and restless. It sounds like you're not doing what your heart wants."

She whined, "But I don't *know* what my heart wants!"

"Well, I imagine your heart knows! What are your interests or favorite things to do?"

"I love yoga, going for runs, cooking good food, and hanging out with my girlfriends. I love traveling—we've been to Europe, Southeast Asia, and Greece. It's been awesome." Her face darkened. "But it's been hard too. Sometimes we see such poverty... It breaks my heart when I see women and children on the streets. I wish there was something I could do to help them. The world should be more fair."

"What would you do to help them?"

"I don't know... They should have education, good jobs... But first, they need healthcare. They've got sores on their bodies, they're malnourished, they've got diseases. If they could get access to vaccines and good maternal healthcare, it would make a huge difference in their life. I see it all the time in the ER..." She began squirming in her seat, her voice rising with excitement. "The doctors rush in...saving lives, delivering babies... They diagnose painful conditions and give medications that clear it up in just a few days! Doctors give people a new lease on life! Their work is so important and meaningful; they really enable people to have a good life."

Getting an inkling that we were onto something, I asked, "Have you ever considered going into medicine?"

She balked. "What?!... Oh, no! I could never do that! I'm not smart enough… and I don't have that kind of money... Besides, it takes *years* to be a doctor."

"And yet, you lit up when you were talking about the doctors working in the ER...giving people a 'new lease on life.' Out of curiosity, what were your grades like in school?"

"I got As, except when I was seeing you. My grades dropped then, but I pulled them out. School was pretty easy for me. But I've never thought of being a doctor—that's *way* out there! Besides, no one in my family has ever been in medicine."

I smiled brightly. "Well, maybe you could be the first!"

Clarise was pretty sure medicine wasn't in her future, but she was definitely being drawn toward something new. As she said, her current job was feeling "kinda rote." Perhaps if we cleared some of her barriers, she could land on what was calling her.

Over the next few weeks, we worked to release the fears and the limiting beliefs that were getting in her way. We cleared a little girl who didn't think she was "smart enough." We released her fears related to money, and we cleared a teenage formation who believed that she had to live out the same script that her family was living. I also helped Clarise reconnect with her Essence so she would have stability and clarity when it came time to recognize her path. With her fears cleared, Clarise was ready to take a deep dive to ask the important questions that would open her life.

"So, for today's session, we're asking the question, 'What is Clarise meant to be doing with her life?' Why don't you close your eyes and get mindful, and we'll start with some easy questions." Clarise closed her eyes and snuggled into the cushions.

"Now, if you were in the 'right' life or 'right' job, what do you imagine it would feel like?"

With her eyes closed, she smiled. "Hmmm! It would be fun... satisfying...meaningful...challenging enough to be interesting...and it would definitely involve helping people."

"Okay... And what domains would you be focused on? Would it be a physical job...a job where you use your intellect..."

She wrinkled her nose. "It wouldn't be a physical job, like being a physical therapist or anything. And it wouldn't be an emotional job, like being a psychotherapist." She flinched. "No offense to you! I just don't want to be a therapist."

Kindly, I said, "No offense taken! I wouldn't want you to be a therapist unless that's what your heart desires. So, it's not a physical job or an emotional job... How about the Cognitive Domain—maybe an intellectual job?"

"I do like figuring things out. Maybe I could do something to help people get healthy, like those women and children I saw on the streets when I was traveling. I would love it if I could help them… It would be fun to have a clinic where they could come and get treated and I could..." She gasped, bursting into tears. *"And I could be their doctor!"* She was laughing and crying all at once, covering her mouth as if she couldn't believe what had just come out of it. Catching her breath, she opened her eyes and stared at me intensely, as if I was her anchor for this new identity. I smiled warmly at her. After a few shaky breaths, she said the words again, this time, claiming it: "I want to be a doctor...and I want to work with women and children!"

"Congratulations, Clarise! You figured it out! All it took was clearing some fears and connecting to your Essence so you could hear your heart!" She nodded, still working to catch her breath.

"Why don't you take some long, deep breaths to help you integrate this new insight. Breathe out any tension and fear, and imagine yourself in a big river valley or a natural space—some place big enough to hold this new awareness." She closed her eyes and took some deep breaths, exhaling slowly.

When her breathing became steady, I asked, "How are you doing?"

With her eyes closed, she smiled. "I'm sitting on a big beach; it feels nice."

"Great. So, as you're imagining yourself sitting on this big beach, allow yourself to settle into the idea of being a doctor."

I waited quietly, watching as her breaths deepened and became more easeful. When she settled, she opened her eyes, smiling. "This feels right. I feel like I just 'landed.'"

I smiled back. "Do you remember when you graduated from college, I told you that you don't plan your life, you *discover* your life?" She nodded. "Well, you just discovered the next chapter, a beautiful path that speaks to your heart and soul."

She smiled, nodding, then suddenly looked anxious. "This is scary! This is a BIG deal."

I nodded reassuringly. "It *is* a big deal. Opening to a new life can feel scary, but you can learn to grow comfortable with the changes and growth. With every new integration, we step into a new identity. Once, you were a college graduate, then a working professional, now you get to be a medical student, and then a doctor... Then there will be other integrations—you may marry or decide not to. You may decide to become a parent. Maybe you'll move to Southeast Asia. Each integration will bring you closer to your True Nature, who you were born to be. Becoming a doctor will take lots of hard work and commitment, but when you're doing what you love, living out your passions, life feels joyful and fulfilling, no matter how long it takes."

When Clarise had walked into my office a month earlier, she had all the pieces lined up for her discovery: Her domains were generally healthy. She was smart, she worked at a hospital, and she clearly loved the rush and stimulation of medicine. She was also drawn to helping women and children. But these pieces couldn't integrate into a clear vision because of her limiting beliefs. With the release of her fears and connecting to her Essence, along with some mindful reflection, the conditions were right for the pieces to fuse together... *Bellissima! She wants to be a doctor!*

When clarity hits, it can be intense as we find ourselves suddenly standing in a new life: *I'm done with this job! I'm gay! I'm moving to New York! I want to have children! I'm leaving this marriage.* Our insight can leave us reeling—we may laugh with joy at our newfound freedom, or cry because our old life is over. Sometimes we laugh and cry at the same moment, just as Clarise did. When our new life appears, it can be both exhilarating and scary as we discover ourselves standing on the edge of new territory.

Other times integration comes quietly, like the slow dawning of a sunrise. In our mind and heart, a secret knowing takes hold, and in that moment, everything changes—knowing what we know, we cannot turn back: *I won't compromise my values for this company, even if I get fired.* We may cross a threshold, suddenly claiming a new identity: *Oh wow! I'm a FATHER!* We may realize something we never understood until this moment: *You're never coming back, are you?* Or we may embrace an outcome that we have been avoiding: *I'm not doing any more cancer treatments. I'm done.* Whether our insight comes as a thunder bolt or a quiet whisper, True Nature has spoken, and our life will never be the same. Like Clarise, we might need to do some quiet breathing on an imaginary beach to integrate our insight before we move onto our new life.

> Integration is not a "one and done" thing. It is an ongoing, rolling process that continues throughout our lifetime.

Integration is not a "one and done" thing. It is an ongoing, rolling process that continues throughout our lifetime. We realize a truth, take a few steps to enact our new insight, and usually bump up against some fears and limitations. With the release of our old pain, fear, and doubt, we can settle into our Essence and cultivate our domains to realize our new dreams and aspirations. We then live with this identity for a while, and then new aspirations appear; and the whole process begins again, taking us closer and closer to our True Nature: *This is what I was born to do!* Coming home to our True Nature makes life fun and inspiring.

As you reflect on your life, do you have anything that is "gnawing" at you? You may feel called to a bigger life, but you don't know exactly what it is. Perhaps something is "off" in your life—a relationship, a job, or some family dynamic—you can't quite put your finger on it, but you know that something's not right. Maybe you've been dreaming about a new job or an adventure, but it seems out of reach. If so, there's a good chance that you are struggling with a challenge of integration. To set things right, take a wholistic view of your situation: Reflect on your issue through the lens of the Seven Domains and the Eight Determinants (Chapters One and Six). In doing so, you'll locate the domains that are not being fully expressed. As you delve into your explorations, you may find some fearful beliefs or old scripts that are holding you back. You may realize that you need additional development and cultivation to actualize your dreams. You may need to make some changes to your environment, or bring in additional supports to help you achieve your aspirations. When you take an *integrated approach* to your life—exploring your issues, projects, and dreams through a wholistic perspective, you increase the likelihood of success in any endeavor.

> When you take an *integrated approach* to your life—exploring your issues, projects, and dreams through a wholistic perspective, you increase the likelihood of success in any endeavor.

Thriving in Personal and Social Competence

The Integrative Domain is the wellspring of what Mark and I call "Personal and Social Competence," a hallmark of True Success. *Competence* is a measure of effective performance. When we are "competent," we are able to apply our skills, knowledge, and attributes in effective ways in order to fulfill our tasks and obligations successfully.

Personal competence speaks to how well we sustain our health and well-being across our domains. When we have personal competence, we can be counted on to act in effective, rational ways when it comes to our health, our work, and our personal expression. We know how to lean into our strengths, and we are capable of developing any areas of personal weakness. When we are personally competent, we live with a sense of clarity and authenticity—we know ourselves, we embrace our unique qualities, and we follow our passions. When we do encounter difficulties, we hold ourselves accountable and take care of ourselves with kindness and wisdom.

Social competence speaks to how well we function in relation to others. Here, our domains integrate to support healthy, social interactions. When we are socially competent, we meet others in ways that are effective and helpful. We endeavor to make others feel at ease and offer a sense of belonging. We listen respectfully to others and welcome civil discourse, encouraging others to share different views so we can enhance our wisdom and understanding. With social competence, we work to let go of our fears and hinderances so we can "show up" in our intimate relationships, offering integrity, kindness, empathy, and support. And when we encounter conflict in relationships, we meet those challenges thoughtfully and open heartedly, recognizing them as opportunities for growth. When we have strong social competence, we make positive contributions to our community and the world.

Personal and Social Competence is a key component of True Success. When we possess Personal and Social Competence, we meet life in adaptive, wise, skillful ways, creating the best opportunities for successful outcomes, both for ourselves and others. Personal and Social Competence is not about striving for perfection, but rather it is the unification of our psychological, emotional, physical, social, cognitive, and spiritual wisdom empowering us to become thoughtful, well-balanced individuals who are comfortable

> When we possess Personal and Social Competence, we meet life in adaptive, wise, skillful ways, creating the best opportunities for successful outcomes, both for ourselves and others.

expressing the Success Traits. Personal and Social Competence is the hallmark of great leaders, healthy parents, effective team members, and strong communities. With Personal and Social Competence, we bring the Success Traits into all our encounters.

Creating a Truly Successful World

As we begin to live more successfully, we may find that living a pleasant life is not fully satisfying. Like Clarise, we may be drawn to making a positive difference in our world. As we become more aware of our interconnectedness with the whole world, we begin to understand that a truly successful life extends far beyond our own happiness.

In her lifelong work on *Active Hope*, Joanna Macy tells us that we each have our own unique way of making contributions to our world. Our world needs lots of love and care, but we don't have to fix everything. Like Clarise, we simply do what our heart is called to do. As Joanna Macy explains, our personal passions often fall into one of three kinds of service: *Upholding Actions, Shifts in Consciousness*, and *Structural Change*. Together, these offerings have the power to heal and renew our world.

As we reflect on how we might benefit the world, some of us will feel called to Upholding Actions—these are deeds that focus on addressing harm as it occurs in our world. Inspired to alleviate suffering, we may become lawyers, activists, rescue workers, police officers, doctors, or the mom who stands up at the school board meeting to address bullying in the schools. These are the people who work passionately to keep us safe and protect us from the fallout of harmful events.

Others are called to create Shifts in Consciousness—offering ideas and practices that open our minds to new ways of thinking that support healthy, sustainable living. These are our teachers, psychotherapists, spiritual leaders, independent film makers, writers, and family members who expand our view of ourselves and the world, so we can let go of our outdated beliefs and embrace new evolving viewpoints that invite healthy, vibrant living.

And there are those who love to build Structural Change, creating new structures and systems that allow us to live in healthy, adaptive ways. These are our engineers, designers, programmers, leaders, and community members who have the skills and means to build the technology, infrastructure, housing, medicines, and other amenities that provide for healthy, sustainable living.

As you reflect on these classifications—Upholding Actions, Creating Shifts in Consciousness, Building Structural Change—do you find yourself called to a particular corner? Which of these roles excites your heart? As Joanna Macy points out, to make a positive contribution, we don't have to "do it all," we just have to follow the passions of our heart, do what is ours to do, and make our corner of the world a little more successful. Every act of kindness, support, and love has a positive impact—when we drop a pebble of kindness or wisdom into the world, it ripples out, bringing us closer to a more successful world.

As we clear our limiting beliefs and embody our True Nature, we can take these Active Hope offerings to their fullest potential. Empowered by our Essence and the integrated wisdom of our domains, we can see the "bigger" picture, we're grounded in strength and wisdom, we're nonreactive, and we are governed by compassion, all of which enables us to make wiser, more empathic choices when we are engaged in our passions and service. With a mind and heart imbued with Essence, we bring great care and wisdom to parenting our children...relating with our families...interacting at work...caring for our animals...engaging with our community...and navigating critical issues such as climate change, globalization, and the global economy. When we are acting from our True Nature, we have everything we need to create a loving, sustainable world—a truly successful world.

In one of her famous poems, Mary Oliver asks, "What will you do with your one wild and precious life?" When we discover our True Nature, we begin a journey to answer that question. In our True Nature, our inner compass points "true north," in the direction of a meaningful and fulfilling life. Your True Nature may shine when you are programming, designing projects, or conducting experiments. You may radiate when you're parenting or making lasagna for your neighbors. You may sparkle anytime you are gardening, singing, creating art, or dancing. You may feel fully alive when you are advocating for passions and causes, or when you're saving the planet. However you express your one wild and precious life, may you find the meaning and fulfillment that comes with living your *True Nature*.

True Success For All

Living our True Nature, as best we can,
right here in this moment, and helping others do the same.

TRUE SUCCESS

Acknowledgments

The book you hold in your hands has been lovingly crafted with the help of many people. I am grateful for the wise, thoughtful guidance of my editor, Shoshana Alexander. Seeing the vision of this book, she brought her keen insights, brilliance, and editing talents to these pages, honing its message and encouraging me to express myself fully and vulnerably. I am also grateful for those who offered their time to read my manuscript and offer feedback—their wisdom is also reflected in these pages. Special thanks to Joan Cyr, Lauren Manasse, and Patrick Latham who scrutinized many variations of the book as the writing progressed. Many thanks to the publishing team of DartFrog Books for their wisdom and support in bringing this book to life.

I am grateful to family and friends who have supported me through the writing of this book, and to the mentors, teachers, colleagues, and instructors who have taught me, supervised me, held me, and guided me, honing my fiery passion into a warm flame of service. Thank you to James Baraz, Carol Mostow, Cedar Barstow, Valeta Bruce, Katherine Barr, Nattalie Blau, Colin Smith, Lauren Manasse, Theresa Carson, Deborah Cyr, Joan Cyr, Cecilia Talamantes, John Gentry, Cecile Fraley, Jamie Knight, Kathleen Gariboldi, and Nanci Edgcomb, your presence in my life has made me a better person.

My deepest thanks go to my husband and partner, Mark. His bright, expansive vision, along with his love and care for the world's well-being and health has inspired many of the ideas and frameworks presented in this book. I am blessed to share my life and this work with my Best Friend and Love. Thank you, Mark, for all your support in writing this book, I couldn't have done it without you! And I lovingly offer deep gratitude to my children for their patience, understanding, wisdom, and support over these many years as I developed this book. I tried to keep a healthy balance between mother and writer—I hope I succeeded. May this endeavor inspire you both to pursue your passions and dreams.

About the Author

Maureen Fallon-Cyr, LCSW, is a graduate of Smith College School for Social Work and a certified Hakomi Therapist. For more than 30 years, she has brought mindfulness-based psychotherapy to people of all ages, specializing in trauma, somatic release and depth psychology. Maureen also served on the teaching council of the Durango Dharma Center for eight years, teaching classes in meditation, mindful parenting, mindfulness 12-Step work, and compassionate living.

Together, with her husband, Mark Fallon-Cyr, M.D., they have brought their 30 years of experience treating children, families, and adults, as well as consulting to numerous educational and health organizations to develop *True Success for All*, a model of self-discovery that empowers people to reimagine what successful living looks like. In workshops and classes, they offer practices that help people develop fresh skills and build strong competency across their life—in work, in relationships, and in manifesting their dreams and potential. When they are not working or teaching True Success, Maureen and Mark enjoy living in Colorado, where they play in the mountains and spend time with family and friends.

Learn more at www.truesuccessforall.com.

Sources

American Time Use Survey—2019. Bureau of Labor Statistics. (2022, June 22). Retrieved October 13, 2022. https://www.bls.gov/news.release/pdf/atus.pdf.

Hilmers, A., Hilmers, D. C., & Dave, J. M. "Neighborhood Disparities in Access to Healthy Foods and Their Effects on Environmental Justice." American Journal of Public Health, 102(9), 1644–1654. (2012). https://doi.org/10.2105/ajph.2012.300865.

News-Medical.net, & Henderson, B.Sc. E. "Low-income Families Have High Awareness of Healthy Diets But Can't Afford Good Quality Food." News-Medical.net. (2021, February 24). Retrieved May 8, 2021. https://www.news-medical.net/news/20210224/Low-income-families-have-high-awareness-of-healthy-diets-but-cant-afford-good-quality-food.aspx.

Pedersen, T. "All About Somatic Therapy." Psych Central. (2021, August 18). https://psychcentral.com/blog/how-somatic-therapy-can-help-patients-suffering-from-psychological-trauma.

Mayo Clinic. "Sitting Risks: How Harmful Is Too Much Sitting?" (2022, July 13). https://www.mayoclinic.org/healthy-lifestyle/adult-health/expert-answers/sitting/faq-20058005.

World Health Organization: WHO. "Obesity and Overweight." (2021). www.who.int.   https://www.who.int/news-room/fact-sheets/detail/obesity-and-overweight.

A Beginner's Guide to MI — MI Oasis. (n.d.). MI Oasis. https://www.multipleintelligencesoasis.org/a-beginners-guide-to-mi.

Hunt, E., PhD. "Improving Intelligence." *Psychology Today.* (2013, February 6). Retrieved April 6, 2020. https://www.psychologytoday.com/us/blog/exploring-intelligence/201302/improving-intelligence.

Dweck, C., PhD. *The New Psychology of Success.* Ballentine Books, 2016.

Dweck, C. (n.d.). "The Power of Believing That You Can Improve" [Video]. TED Talks. https://www.ted.com/talks/carol_dweck_the_power_of_believing_that_you_can_improve.

Wurr, L. "Can Stress at Work Affect Cognitive Performance?" *Cambridge Cognition.* (2023). https://www.cambridgecognition.com/blog/entry/can-stress-at-work-affect-cognitive-performance.

www.ingramcontent.com/pod-product-compliance
Lightning Source LLC
Chambersburg PA
CBHW061146120626
46546CB00005B/1951